100 Life Lessons I've Learned So You Don't Have To

by Rosally Saltsman

100 Life Lessons I've Learned So You Don't Have To
by Rosally Saltsman
First published 2022
ISBN: 978-1-56871-694-7

Copyright © Rosally Saltsman

Published by:
Targum Publishers
Shlomo ben Yosef 131a/1
Jerusalem 9380581
Israel
info@targumpublishers.com

Layout: Nechama Harkavy
Copy Editor: Farla Klaiman

All rights reserved

IN MEMORY OF

my parents

חנה בת קלמן

משה לייזר בן ברוך

and my uncle

ישראל בן קלמן

my son's father

גרשון חיים בן זליג אברהם

my paternal grandparents

דב ברוך בן חמיה

שיינדל

my maternal grandparents

רוזה נחמה בת זרח

קלמן בן ישראל

זיכרונם לברכה
May they all have an *illui neshamah*

Take words with you and return to Hashem.

HOSHEA 14:3

Behold, I have come with the scroll of the book written about me.

TEHILLIM 40:8

The great thing about getting older is that you don't lose all the other ages you've been.

MADELEINE L'ENGLE CAMP

Table Of Contents

Preface 12

Acknowledgments 13

Nishmat Kol Chai 16

Rich in Romania 18

Missing Home 20

Reflections of You and Me 22

I Am a Squirrel 25

Shall We Dance?! 27

Just a Little Bit 29

Just a Little Bit II 31

Vitamin Deficiency 33

MESSages! 34

Backstage Baby 36

We Can Be the Light 38

A Little Light 40

Just Ask 42

Bully for You 44

One Kind Word 46

Just Pray for It 48

Who Knows? 50

Five Minutes of Fame 53

Bearing the Guilt 55

Coming Home 57

The Height of Observation	61
A Bit of a Vice	63
Fanatastic	66
Master of Our Destiny	69
The Name of the Game	73
Drawing Closer	75
The King's Emissary	77
Remembering Uncle George	79
Leah's Luncheon	81
What Goes Around, Comes Around	83
Welcome to Rosality	85
Day of Judgment	87
The Secret to Happiness	89
Roughing It	94
Why Nothing Ever Works	97
Your Own Thing	99
On Impact	102
For Whom the Cock Crows	104
Time Is of the Essence	106
Flight of the Phoenix	108
Par for the Course	110
A Valuable Lesson	111
Into the Arena	114
Mirror Image	117
The Cat's Meow	119
A Friend in Need	121

Back in the Saddle	123
Hashem's Got My Back	125
The Spiritual Down Side	127
The Bigger They Are	129
On the Job	131
About Face	133
String Theory	135
Betta Believe It	137
To Shield and Protect	139
Picture This	142
Interdisciplinary Decisions	144
For the Birds	146
Dichotomy	148
Stress and the City	150
Senses and Sensibility	153
A Very Good Point, Miss Saltsman	155
Global Positioning Spiritually	157
Divine Choreography	159
Nahafochu	160
Matters	164
God Is with Me	167
Life Is in the Details	169
The Elixir of Encouragement	171
Habitat	173
Climbing Maslow's Pyramid	175
An Infusion of Praise	178

Choices	180
Spiritual IQ	183
Lost in Translation	185
Harav Kook vs. Don Quixote	187
Making Contact	188
Ricki's List	191
Mistress of Finance	192
Going Overboard	194
Seeking Forgiveness	196
The Tipping Point	201
Noteworthy Friends	204
Slippery Slope	207
Taken for a Ride	209
Independence Day	212
While I Was Sleeping	213
Heartfelt Prayer	216
Incognito	217
The Meaning of Life Is Cuddling	219
Thomas and Friends	221
Glimpses from Beyond	223
Driving Test	225
The Play's the Thing	228
Hard to Admit	231
Let It Rain	234
Tears on My Pillow	236
From a Different Perspective	238

Zoology..241

Dress Code..243

Fame and Anonymity..245

In the Pink..247

Pyramid Scheme..249

Glossary..251

Please Note:
Unattributed quotes in this book are either anonymous or written by me.

This book contains words of Torah. Please do not take it into the bathroom, lay it on the floor, or dispose of it anywhere but in a *genizah* (receptacle for books containing scripture).

Differences in spelling (pronunciation) of Hebrew, Yiddish or Aramaic words or expressions are deliberate.

There is a glossary at the end of the book for the above.

These stories span six decades and I have chosen not to present them chronologically or even thematically. I apologize for any confusion this might cause.

Preface

Out of the Box

Nothing is impossible; the word itself says 'I'm possible'!
AUDREY HEPBURN

I spent the first ten days of my life in an incubator, having been born two months premature. Since then, I have been thinking out of the box.

Life is made up of lessons and the more types of experience you're open to, the more lessons you learn.

This book is a compilation of some of those experiences and some of those lessons. I share them with you in the hope that they will help you in your life's curriculum.

Acknowledgments

A psalm of thanksgiving. Call out to Hashem, everyone on earth.

TEHILLIM 100:1

Although the literal meaning of the above verse is that everyone on earth should give thanks to Hashem, it could also be read as stating that we each should give thanks to Hashem and also to everyone on earth. It seems that everyone on earth has had some input into our existence, especially now that the world is a global village and we are all connected in so many ways. Everyone who has come before us, and everyone who has come in contact with us, has surely had some effect on who we have become.

But in keeping with the plain meaning of the verse, I thank God first for life, for sustenance, for the many blessings He has given me (sometimes in disguise and sometimes beyond my wildest expectations), and for every day I have lived. My mother died when she was fifty-seven years old, so when I reached that age, I got a bit nervous that perhaps I too had reached the end of my sojourn on earth. But thank God, I made it to the Mishnah's definition of old age — sixty — and am still going, *baruch Hashem*. So I'm grateful for that.

My parents, of course, gave me life, and from what I understood, it took a while. I am an only child (for better or worse), my mother liked to joke that I was made in Japan (seriously; my parents were on a world tour), and during the course of my mother's pregnancy, she had brain surgery. I was born two months premature and spent ten days in an incubator. So I guess I was a challenging child from the beginning.

I owe a sincere debt of gratitude to all my spiritual guides and advisors, who illuminated my path whether as friends, religious leaders, teachers, or role models.

I was named after both my grandmothers Rosa and Sheindel, which translated to Rosally in English and Shoshana Yaffa (a beautiful rose) in Hebrew, so I thank them for being their namesake.

I realize I am but a link in the chain of my personal and national history and that I owe my place to everyone who has come before me and everyone to follow.

My Uncle Issey was a formative figure in my childhood. He lived with us for several years. He died when I was only nine years old. There is no question that aside from fond memories, he contributed much to my growing up. He was also a writer, and I can't help feeling that that had something to do with my becoming one.

My late ex-husband gave me the most precious gift — our son, Josh, *ad* 120! Although Gordon only lived till Josh was fourteen, he's *shepping* (receiving) a lot of *naches* (pride and joy) in Heaven, I'm sure. And I will be forever grateful to him.

My son is my greatest treasure and I thank him for being in my life and being such a wonderful son, *bli ayin hara*.

I have been fortunate to have many friends in the different chapters of my life and the many places I have lived. It has always pained me to lose a friendship, but I have recently comforted myself with the thought that our lives are like a train journey, in the course of which many people get on and off at the various stations where the train stops. They accompany us on part of our journey and then continue with their own. Nevertheless, I have been blessed with several amazing friends who have been with me for most of the ride, and I am grateful to have them with me on this scenic and sometimes adventurous trip. You know who you are, and I am grateful to you for sticking with me all these years and enriching my life in myriad ways!

I thank my many friends across the world for your contribution to my life. The stories in this book do not pay homage to or even mention many of them. But they have all had a deep and lasting influence on my life and I dare not name them all for fear of forgetting one.

I thank the editors who have allowed me to grace the pages of their periodicals and to use many of those articles here — most notably Rebbetzin Sheindel Weinbach, Naomi Mauer, Chana Weisberg, and Dan Levy.

I thank Nechama Harkavy for the wonderful job she's done laying out the book.

A heartfelt thank you to Badia, who recently made it possible for me not only to review my life but to come to terms with many parts of it. We all need guides in this life and she is one of those angels.

Acknowledgments

I thank my beta readers, and those who graciously agreed to offer kind words about this book. And, as always, my chief copyeditor, and great friend, Farla Klaiman.

Last but not least, you the reader have given me the incentive to hope that, in some way, I will be able to inspire, touch, amuse, entertain, or move you. I hope I have not been misguided in my attempts. I share with you my stories because it is those experiences that we have in common and can share with one another, hopefully for mutual enlightenment that will help us in our personal journey to bring more light and love into the world, and to grow and make the difference God put us in this world to make.

Thank you all!

Rosally

Nishmat Kol Chai

Making the decision to have a child is momentous. It is to decide forever to have your heart go walking around outside your body.

ELIZABETH STONE

When I was twenty-five years old, I was in a major car accident that totaled the car and landed me in the hospital. The first question I asked, after ascertaining that everyone was okay - *baruch Hashem* (thank God), they were - was if I would still be able to have children. I was barely conscious but my maternal instinct was faring well. Thank God, my only injuries were mild and would have no bearing on my procreative abilities.

When I was thirty-one years old, I became a mother. It was amazing how quick the transformation was and how suddenly my only thought, care and worry was for the small human being I had just given birth to. I remember when they took him away to do whatever they do with new babies, that I refused to go into my room until they brought him back. Everyone at the hospital, including the other mothers, asked me if this was my first child. I was wondering, "Why? Do you stop caring so much after the first one?" I never found out; he's my only baby.

The next morning (or the same morning actually) I felt overwhelmed with a desire to give thanks for my beautiful baby boy. I went up to a woman in the cafeteria (this was a religious hospital – Mayanei Hayeshua, the Spring of Salvation – in Bnei Brak) and asked her what prayer of thanksgiving you say after giving birth to a child. She told me to say the *Nishmat Kol Chai* prayer. I did. And now every Shabbat when I say it, I think back to that morning, when I thanked God for the gift of a child, for the gift of motherhood. I named my son Yehoshua Yisrael (God saves Israel) after two of his great uncles, but it's only now that I think how the name of my son is connected to the name of the hospital.

That feeling of overflowing with gratitude isn't one we experience all the time. But it should be. Because every moment we're alive, we're being gifted with life along with all the blessings we enjoy in our lives – family, friends, children, sustenance, water, oxygen…

The time we are most cognizant of our blessings is of course when we first receive them – standing under the *chuppah* (bridal canopy), the births or adoption of our children, graduation (our degrees), a windfall, our first job or house - but the fact is that we should be thanking God for them all the time. It's obviously hard to maintain that high level of gratitude all the time, but the truth is every second we enjoy our blessings, God's gifts and the gifts bestowed on us by others, we should be feeling and expressing gratitude.

We have relegated times to express gratitude – the High Holidays, *simchahs* (celebrations), birthdays, *seudot hodayah* (feasts of thanksgiving) and holidays, are when we thank God and show *hakarat hatov* (gratitude). Like the *Nishmat* prayer says, however, we would never ever be able to express the gratitude we need to show for all our blessings even if our mouth was as full of song as the sea and our lips as full of praise as the breadth of the heavens.

As much as we can, let us embrace an attitude of gratitude to Hashem and to others, and live with the joy that every moment of every day brings.

I dedicate this book to my amazing and wonderful son, Yehoshua Yisrael (Josh) Geller, *nero yair* (may his light shine), *ad* (till) -120, for whom I have felt (and hopefully shown) the most gratitude. He has taught me the most valuable of life's lessons and is also a great teacher.

הודו לה' כי טוב. כי לעולם חסדו!
Give thanks to Hashem, for He is good, for His kindness endures forever!

This also appears in Eternally Grateful.

Rich in Romania

[Regarding the lifestyle of the people of Romania] I learned how little in the way of material goods we really need, and how beautiful a simple life can be. In Romania people work with their hands every day, and you'll see an eighty-year-old woman still chopping wood because she's been looking after herself all her life, and she still has the strength to do it.

RENÉE ZELLWEGER

In December of 1989, I visited Romania. People lived in such primitive and deprived conditions that I kept asking why they didn't revolt. Someone must have heard me because two weeks later, they did.

On my first day there, I changed money on the black market; that is someone gave me a lot of *lei* for one hundred American dollars. A lot of *lei*! It was the most currency I had ever seen in one place. There was only one problem with it. There was nothing to buy. Nicolae Ceaușescu's government had left Romanians living in poverty with empty shelves in their stores and no produce in their markets. It was like nothing I had ever experienced. I hadn't counted on it being so cold and I had to go to several stores to find one pair of gloves. I think someone just gave me a pair.

Whereas usually there was a lot to be had but I didn't have the money to buy much, now I had lots of money but there was nothing to buy. I was the richest I had ever been, relatively speaking, and if I could only find it, I could buy anything I wanted.

I remember going for a pedicure and tipping the person more than it cost. It was a wonderful feeling but it was a bittersweet triumph. What's the good of having all this money if you couldn't buy anything?

Buying power is one way we judge if someone's rich. Possessions are another way. But it's all relative. All I had was a hundred dollars' worth of *lei* but it was a virtual fortune in downtrodden Romania at the time.

When we say we want a lot of money, we usually mean we want what the money can afford us. And when we say that, we usually mean whatever is available to everyone else. The potential to get whatever I wanted, the opposite of a feeling of lack was what made the difference.

I was feeling rich, simply because I had more buying power than anyone else, even though there was almost nothing to buy. Hot water, heating, light, food - all these were in poor supply in Romania at the time. Was I really richer than I am now with sufficient food, heating, light, even though I can't afford a car or a trip abroad?

I didn't mind; it was an adventure. But was it really so much fun to be above everyone else's poverty and discontent?

It was a lot like having Monopoly money. I had to get rid of it before I left Romania because you couldn't take money out of the country. It was like being on one of those spending sprees where you had to spend as much as you can in a given time limit.

I often wonder what happened to the people I met and how they fared through the revolution. I've heard that since that time, Romania has experienced an improvement in lifestyle and greater freedom. My vacation there put a lot of my ideas about having money and the things they can buy into perspective. And I became the richer for it, in more ways than one.

Reprinted from The Money Book

Missing Home

The way of the world is such that parents feel the pain of their children, but the children are oblivious to the suffering of their parents. Likewise, God feels our pain, but we are blind to His misery.

RABBI MENACHEM MENDEL OF KOTZK

My son went to visit his father and his family in California. He was away for over two weeks, seven thousand miles, and oceans away. My son till-120, was going to be fourteen and we'd only been separated for a few days in all that time. It was difficult (single mother, only child). I was pining.

Although my son did miss me and home, he was a bit distracted. Disneyland, the pool, Pizza World, and Universal Studios diverted his attention from homesickness and, in his own right, he was a celebrity (as a son, grandchild, nephew, cousin visiting from Israel).

Although it was difficult for me, I let him go because I knew it would be fun and good for him. That's the way of the world. You teach your children to fly and then you let them. Of course seven thousand miles is a bit far. Thank God he came back safely and I breathed more freely again.

This was one of those times when my mother's *a"h* (may her memory be for a blessing) exhortation of, "Just wait until you're a mother," rang true. I never understood why she made such a big deal when I went away. I do now.

Although we're not supposed to envision God in human form, we are offered a number of analogies regarding our relationship to Him. One of those is a father (or a mother - the *Shechinah*) and child.

When the *Beit Hamikdash* (Temple) was destroyed, God's children went into exile (yes, even those of us living in Israel) and now not only is the *Shechinah* (God's presence in its feminine form) without a home, she is bereft and her grief is echoed in the heartrending cries of Rachel for her children.

Of course, we, God's children, long to return both physically to our Homeland, to the *Beit Hamikdash*, may it be built speedily and soon, and spiritually to our Father in Heaven. But we tend to get a bit distracted. Most of today's Jews live in comfort and affluence in North America, Australia, New Zealand, South Africa, South America, and Europe. The material level of Jews today is like never before and it sometimes slips our minds, while we lounge in our mini sanctuaries, and go about our daily lives, that the *Shechinah* is homeless and Hashem is anxious for our return to Him.

God doesn't begrudge us material comforts or Disneyland, but He wants us to remember who we are, why we're here and Who truly loves us. We shouldn't get so distracted by the "delights" of our exile that we forget to want to come home.

It's time for us to reassess our priorities, redefine our identities and express our desire for closeness with God.

When my son returned home, he was bubbling over with his experiences, happy to have had them but, more importantly, happy to be home. I could tell he had missed me too.

Next year, it is quite likely that if he wants to go back for another visit, I would let him and endure the time we are separated waiting for him to come home.

But wouldn't it be even better if by next year *Mashiach* (the Messiah) has come, and every Jew in America has moved here, to Israel, and the biggest attraction in the world will be the *Beit Hamikdash*?

Well, maybe even if that comes to pass, God willing, my son would want to go to America. But then, I'd have a place to go offer a sacrifice of thanksgiving when he, *b'ezrat Hashem* (God willing), comes home safely.

Let us all *b'ezrat Hashem* return Home safely.

First published in The Jewish Press

Reflections of You and Me

As water reflects a face back to a face, so one's heart is reflected back to him by another.

MISHLEI 27:19

I had to catch a 6:13 a.m. train to Modi'in from Petach Tikvah, otherwise I would miss the bar mitzvah. Some places have transportation between them every five minutes. With others the frequency ranges from hours to days. So I showed up at the train station at a quarter to six. It was locked. I asked the guard when they would be opening. He said, "Soon."

I said, "But I have a train." True it would take five minutes from the time I entered the station to get to the train, but I like to be early, in plenty of time, you never know.

"Well, what time will you be opening?" I asked.

"I don't know."

You know how everyone has their buttons, their pet peeves, their red capes? Arrogant, uncooperative people who don't comply with a simple request are one of mine. I threatened to complain. He didn't care. Eventually other people arrived and he opened the door, but when I went inside he told me I couldn't come in yet. I refused to move. He threatened to physically evict me. Heated words ensued and I left the station only to be allowed back a minute later. I threatened again. He threatened me with a civil suit if I complained. The cashier at the ticket booth hadn't arrived yet. It was 6:05. The young female guard working with him seemed more reasonable. She said if the cashier didn't come in time, I could go through and pay at the end.

"But why wouldn't he tell me when the station opened?" I asked of her reasonably.

"It depends," she answered sweetly.

"On what?"

"We have regulations."

"But what are the regulations?"

She shrugged.

"I could miss my train!"

"Everything's from Above."

The ticket booth lady had meanwhile arrived and since the train was electric, I was smoking (in anger) in its stead. But a few minutes later, I decided not to complain. It's my job in this world to fix myself, not other people, and I hadn't reacted in a way that made me particularly proud. Also, his attitude, while it provoked and angered me, didn't actually cause any harm. I made the train and the bar mitzvah, both very nice, and the guard didn't actually lay a hand on me. Also since I'm struggling with livelihood myself, I didn't think it was auspicious to threaten someone else's. I decided to let it go.

My trip required me to change trains in Tel Aviv. I was going to get off at the last possible stop, but something made me get off at the central terminal. I had about twenty minutes before my connecting train and sat down on a bench to say *Tehillim* (Psalms).

A bareheaded man, wearing earrings, looking a bit scruffy and smelling of cigarette smoke passed by.

"*Tehillim* is a good thing," he said.

I acknowledged his remark and then called after him, "So say some."

He walked back to me.

"I have a *Tehillim* in my bag but I don't say them." He took out a book to show me.

"Why not?" I asked.

"Because I don't know which to say."

I quickly explained to him how the book was divided into days of the week and days of the month and he decided to say *Tehillim* for the day, which was Thursday.

"I need to cover my head right?" And he rummaged through his bag once more and pulled out an equally scruffy *kippah* (skullcap) and put it awkwardly on his head.

He sat down next to me and we proceeded to say *Tehillim* together in companionable whispers. I felt very Divinely blessed. This was a special moment.

When we finished, I showed him the prayer he could say after each time he recited *Tehillim*. He said he'd say it on the train. He then expressed an interest in learning more. He told me he goes to a *kollel* (yeshiva for married men) every morning where he lays *tefillin* (phylacteries). The *kippah* was obviously scruffy from use. I made a suggestion or two.

We parted with blessings for each other, as the train pulled up.

The man was obviously a Divine emissary - after all something had made me get off at this station, and more than I was teaching him, he was teaching me.

You see the two incidents, the one with the guard and the one with the man, took place half an hour apart. And look what a tremendous difference there was in the interactions.

The Ba'al Shem Tov said that we are all reflections of one another. We show others what they have inside them and they too reflect our flaws and virtues back to us.

We have a possibility at every moment, by our actions and reactions, to inspire others or to bring out their worst. The choice to be, and to see, is ours.

We are all like trains that pass each other on our journeys and stop briefly to make a delivery at each other's stations.

The female guard was right, "Everything *is* from Above!"

First published in The Jewish Press

I Am a Squirrel

Millions of trees in the world are accidentally planted by squirrels, who bury nuts, then forget where they hid them.

A friend of mine told me about a game her daughter and friends played at a wedding shower. Everyone had to say what kind of animal they were. My friend chose a chameleon because she always goes with the flow and knows how to feel comfortable in, and adapt to, every situation. The description actually fit her quite well. So I began to think about what kind of animal I am.

I generally love most animals and the ones I don't "love" I'm fascinated by. When I was a little girl with buckteeth, I strongly resembled a squirrel, as I was also very cute. Or so they told me. When I was sixteen, I had a haircut, which a cousin promptly labeled, "the squirrel." When I was about twenty, I had to meet a woman and give her something in a crowded place. She told me she looked like a goat. I told her I looked like a squirrel. We found each other.

Over the years, I have related to the characteristics of many animals - cats, lions, sloths - but thinking it over, if I had to pick an animal I most relate to, a squirrel still fits the bill. I'm very hyper, even in middle age, and everyone always tells me I move and talk fast. I have little patience and oh yes, I'm still cute, though my cheeks are a little fuller.

I have always berated myself about the fact that I am not an "enjoy the journey" kind of person. Doesn't matter how many of those articles I read about life is a journey, I am very, but very, goal-oriented. I scurry from task to task and leap from project to project, rarely resting on my laurels. This is alternated with periods of hibernation in which I recoup my energy.

After my discussion with my chameleon friend, I was at the aforementioned daughter's wedding and you know what? I didn't try to enjoy it. I had a list of tasks I had to do at the wedding. And for once, although I appreciated the sunset and enjoyed the chopped liver, I didn't feel guilty that I wasn't laid back with no to-do list, because I accepted that I am a squirrel. And without the pressure of trying to live in the moment, I actually had a very good time.

While we all have traits that we need to work on and improve, our natures, our inborn character traits, are meant to be employed in manifesting our true selves and accomplishing what we were put here to do. While some people get annoyed that I'm constantly rushing and under pressure to get things done, making me seem brusque, they also appreciate the fact that I'm energetic, quick and efficient. And if they need someone to leisurely raft down the Mississippi (or Jordan River) with, (though that sounds like fun and something to put on my to-do list), they'll pick someone else.

Humanity is like a prism of color. And when we decorate our lives, sometimes we want subdued tones and sometimes bright ones, sometimes dark deep shades and other times, pale hues. And before anyone writes to tell me that people are multidimensional, and how can I relegate a human being to a zoo exhibit, while we are multi-faceted, multi-dimensional, complex creatures, each of us has a *modus operandi*, a style and rhythm that impacts on a lot of what we do. Yes, I'm deep but I'm also a squirrel.

I urge everyone to take stock of the people in your lives and try to understand them, accept them and love them for who they are. A chicken does not try to be an eagle and neither should it. We each soar to great heights in our own way. And while we're at it, we should love ourselves too, because whatever species we may relate to, we were all created in the Divine image.

Appeared in Binah Magazine

Shall We Dance?!

We learn by practice. Whether it means to learn to dance by practicing dancing or to learn to live by practicing living, the principles are the same. One becomes in some area an athlete of God.

MARTHA GRAHAM

When I was a teenager, I loved musicals. I watched them all the time which made it kind of difficult to adapt to real life, but that's another story.

I heard that one of the medium's more famous stars died and it got me thinking about tap dancing. In my early twenties, when I myself was performing in musicals, I took various kinds of dance classes, one of them being tap. I remember giving it up because it was very painful. In retrospect I think my shoes were too small.

Anyway, as I was looking for exercise I spontaneously decided to buy some tap shoes. Only I ordered them over the Internet and instead of a white pair of size thirty-eight women's shoes, I got a silver pair of size thirty-four girls' shoes. Since it cost as much to get a new pair as it did to return them, and having just read Rebbetzin Sheindel Weinbach's book *Jerusalem Recycled*, I decided to donate them to her *gemach* (free loan society) in Jerusalem as I was planning to visit her anyway, and as it was a month before Purim, maybe it would make some little girl happy. But I didn't give up on the tap shoes yet.

I had plans to meet a friend, who was visiting from Montreal, in Tel Aviv, and decided to go to an Isradance store there. Poetically, I realized that this was the same store where I had bought dance clothes, thirty-five years previously, only it had been refurbished. I was feeling a bit self-conscious but God showed *chesed* (kindness) even here and sent customers around my own age so I'd feel more comfortable. There was a couple who looked to be about my age and the woman was buying character shoes and, as I was paying, another woman walked in looking for a bodysuit. In Hashem's great mercy, I was not surrounded by lithe twenty-something ballerinas and so did not feel totally out of my league. They had a pair of black tap shoes, my size, on sale and so I bought them.

But now where to dance? I tried doing a few steps at home (when my downstairs neighbors were out). I called a couple of dance teachers I knew, looking for a studio to rent for an hour once in a while, but I couldn't find one.

So my new tap shoes are back in my closet. I might not get credit for exercise. But I get lots for all the *hishtadlut* (effort) I did. And a little girl in Jerusalem got a pretty, new pair of silver tap shoes.

First appeared in The Jewish Press

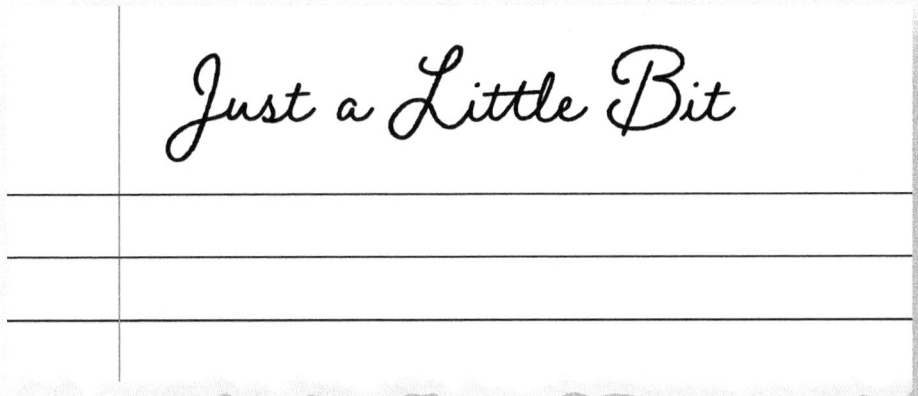

Just a Little Bit

From a song with music by Linda Tomer

Just a little rain
Refreshes the earth
Just a few tears
Clear away the hurt
The tide gently flows
And laps at the sand

Just one little smile
Uplifts the soul
Just one kind word
Can make you feel whole
I can reach high
If you hold out your hand

Just a little bit
It doesn't take much
Just a little bit
A moment, a touch
Just a little bit
Of hope in your heart
For a start

Just a few coins
And they'll feel secure

Believe in their dream
And they can feel sure
A few seconds more
Can last a whole life long

Just a little bit
It doesn't take much
Just a little bit
A moment, a touch
Just a little bit
Of hope in your heart
For a start

Just one deep breath
And you're on your way
A gleam of the eye
So much can convey
Just a few notes
And you've got a song

Just a little bit
It doesn't take much
Just a little bit
A moment, a touch
Just a little bit
Of hope in your heart
For a start

Just one little smile
Uplifts the soul
Just one kind word
Can make you feel whole
I can reach high
If you hold out your hand
You will understand
Just a little bit

Just a Little Bit

Faith is taking the first step, even when you don't see the whole staircase.

MARTIN LUTHER KING, JR.

I was feeling a bit overwhelmed by futility. You know, you try so hard and nothing comes of it. My son had been at a lecture given by Rabbi Eliyahu Godlevsky, the main tenet of whose work is: Be happy with the bit you are able to do. So he told me about it.

Rabbi Godlevsky gave, as an example, a *shiur* (class) he was giving. One of the men who had been a regular (let's call him Moshe) had stopped coming to the *shiur*. This particular night, Moshe decided to attend, but he was running late and considered not attending after all. "What am I going to do for five minutes?" he reasoned. But in the end, he did attend. The class continued for an extra twenty minutes, and so Moshe ended up hearing twenty-five minutes of the lecture.

But that's not all. The Rav (Rabbi) needed a ride, which Moshe happily supplied. Since Moshe was going his way, another member of the *shiur* (let's call him Yaakov) availed himself of the lift. Yaakov asked the Rav if he could give a class in his neighborhood. The Rav said he wasn't able to, but suggested Yaakov buy some discs of his classes. The price was too much for Yaakov to be able to afford, even after the Rav offered him the discs at cost (which is why he was taking lifts and not the bus), so the Rav turned to Moshe and asked if he would be willing to pay for the discs for Yaakov, which he willingly agreed to do. And before the ride was over, Moshe had engaged the Rav to come and give a *shiur* in his neighborhood (as it was closer than Yaakov's).

All this *chesed* and Torah learning had come about because Moshe decided to come to the *shiur* "for only five minutes."

I was walking in downtown Petach Tikvah and there were a few musicians filming a music clip. As they were setting up a shot, one of the musicians (who was leaning against a column, holding a guitar, with a hat in front of him) was obviously annoyed that it was taking so long. Just then, a mother with a few little children in tow, passed by and the children put some coins into the hat. The musician, whose face was immediately transformed by the smile that broke through the cloud on his face, tried to tell the mother that they were only filming. But she insisted that he keep the money, as she and her children walked away smiling. It was seemingly such a small thing, but it totally changed the atmosphere.

That same evening, the sound of children arguing next door reminded me that I had a plate of cakes left over from a *shul* (synagogue) Chanukah party that I wanted to give them. So I knocked on my neighbors' door and watched as a smile spread on the face of the young boy when he realized I was giving him some cake – just a bit of leftover cake.

The next morning, I awoke to an unusual sound. Rain! It was raining! A welcome, albeit short, reprieve from the terrible drought, the worst in a century, that had been plaguing Israel. It provided some relief to the farmers and no doubt raised their spirits, along with the level of the Kinneret, and I'm sure it contributed to ending the days-long battle against the inferno in the North. It was just a bit of rain.

It isn't lost on me that all this happened during Chanukah, a holiday that celebrates the miracle that "just a little bit" can effect. A little bit of oil was found, and we've been celebrating for millennia!

A few minutes, a few coins, a little cake, a bit of rain. Just imagine what else we can accomplish with "just a little bit!"

First published in Hamodia

Vitamin Deficiency

Strength is the ability to break a chocolate bar into four pieces with your bare hands - and then eat just one of those pieces.

JUDITH VIORST

When I was a little girl, my mother made me hot chocolate every morning. And in the hot chocolate (probably on some doctor's recommendation) she put vitamin drops. The vitamins congealed and floated on the top of the hot chocolate as these small misshapen yellow blobs. They were disgusting. Not like the yummy orange-flavored aspirin I sometimes took as a child.

One morning, I came downstairs and there were no yellow globs in my hot chocolate. I was so pleased but assumed my mother had forgotten to put them in. And good girl that I was, I said, "Where are the vitamins?" And that's when my mother told me I didn't have to have them anymore.

And that's when I learned that all unpleasant situations eventually come to an end.

A house is just a place to keep your stuff while you go out and get more stuff.

GEORGE CARLIN

I am a messy person. Moreover, I thrive on mess. If things are too neat, I feel stressed out. Mess shows that I'm doing something with my life. I don't feel comfortable visiting homes that look like they are about to be photographed for a glossy magazine.

A friend was once visiting, a neat friend, and she wondered how I was able to find anything (seriously, it's not that bad). So we played a game. She named an item (scissors, ketchup, a ball…) and I had to find it.

I found each item, every time, within seconds. First of all, mess or no mess, I have a place for everything. You won't find a cat in the refrigerator. That might be because I don't have a cat. But each of my possessions has a permanent abode and if something moves for some reason (like it's currently in use), my mind catalogues that information. I have a photographic memory for my things.

In truth, some of the reason for the mess is that I don't have enough storage space for my stuff. And everyone has too much stuff.

Neat is highly overrated. Because life is messy and your home should reflect that. There are children growing up there, food being prepared, books being read, love being shared, and vestiges of frequent forays into wet and messy weather pooling in the hallway. There are schoolbooks and library books, laundry in various states of being worn and sorted, people getting ready to go out, to go to sleep, to mail letters and exchange gifts. There are instruments being learned and practiced from errant sheet music, sweaters, coats and keys and pictures that need to be put in albums and reminisced over. And papers! Lots and lots of papers - newspapers, magazines, report cards, bills, drawings, notes, and toys and markers. And tools for the vicissitudes of life. And pets, we mustn't forget pets. And crumbs and wrappers and flowers and plants.

If ever it gets too neat in my apartment, and it isn't twenty minutes before candle lighting, or two days before Seder (festive Passover meal), I take some cushions and throw them around, eat a piece of chocolate cake in the living room, make a mess and start celebrating life!

That's a joke - it never gets too neat in my apartment.

Backstage Baby

My body, my life, became the landscape of my son's life. I am no longer merely a thing living in the world; I am a world.
SARAH MANGUSO

It was 1991. I was visiting Montreal from Israel with my beautiful new baby boy. The musical *Phantom of the Opera* was on tour and performing at Place des Arts, a posh, large complex of theaters in downtown Montreal, off the métro stop of the same name.

I really wanted to see *Phantom*, but I was nursing my son and the trip to the theater and back from my childhood home, where I was staying, would take several hours including the performance. Since he was an easy baby, and he loved music, I would often take him with me to musical performances, where he'd enjoy the show while I held him on my lap, but I was afraid the loud dissonant music of some of the songs would prove too overwhelming for this then two-month-old aficionado.

I called a friend and asked her if she would mind coming downtown with me with the baby so I could attend the matinée while she babysat because I really wanted to see this show! She agreed to come but said she didn't feel comfortable hanging around the métro station; could I please find her somewhere to stay in the theater?

So I called the theater, explained my situation and asked if they had a room available where my friend could stay with the baby, while I was attending the performance, which was close enough for me to nurse during intermission. The woman I spoke to in the PR department had apparently never had a request like this before and asked me to call her back in a couple of days while she investigated the possibility. When I did, she said there would be no problem, I should just come early and ask for her.

When the three of us arrived at the theater a few days later, we were escorted up in the VIP elevator and shown into a small first-aid room. My friend told me later that the actors and orchestra cooed over my baby backstage and did their pre-show warm-up entertaining him, a small but captivated, delighted and enraptured audience!

At intermission I bought my friend a *Phantom* souvenir cup and went to my baby who wasn't the least bit hungry, what with all the excitement.

After the show, which was as amazing as anticipated, we were escorted back down in the VIP elevator, avoiding the crowds and the long wait to get out of the parking garage.

It was a memorable matinée for all concerned, my little angel of music and all I asked of Place des Arts.

I ended up nursing for two and a half years and learned to be creative along the way.

We Can Be the Light

From a song with music by Linda Tomer

We are all Stars
Counted in the firmament of Heaven's blessing
Each of our names inscribed in a constellation of love
By the One above

We are all destined to fulfill our path
Like a shooting star
As we go to sleep counting our blessings
Hashem repeats our names

Like a lullaby
Of stars in the sky
We are all blessings
We are all blessings
We are all God's blessings

We can see the light
We can feel the light
We can be the light

Think about your life and all the good within it
Don't dwell on any strife for even half a minute
Each day is rife with opportunities for bliss
Like this
We can see the light

We Can Be the Light

We can see the light
We can feel the light
We can be the light

Think about God's love that everyday surrounds you
Like the summer grass that's draped with morning dew
Think of everything you've got
And everything you're not
It will astound you, like a petal's kiss
And you will see the light

We can see the light
We can feel the light
We can be the light

Each tiny atom making up this universe
Scenarios that seem to go from bad to worse
The milestones that we pass
And each time we raise a glass
A voice in a crystal clear mist whispers
We can see the light

But even more than seeing or basking
And greater still than wanting or asking
With every smile, each step, and deeper insight
We can be the light

We can see the light
We can feel the light
We can be the light

We are all Stars

A Little Light

A little bit of light dispels a lot of darkness.
RABBI SCHNEUR ZALMAN OF LIADI

I was speaking to my oldest and dearest friend, my "adopted sister," Leah. She was talking about how once when I was visiting her in Tzfat, I had made a joke when she tried to slip some garlic into an omelet she was making for us after I had said I didn't want any. She liked how I had made light of it. This friend has known me practically my entire life and this incident took place when we were twenty-three. Of the hundreds of adventures we shared together, this small detail stands out for her.

My late ex-husband once told me that the highlight of our marriage was when I made him come with me to visit Houdini's grave and pray. It's not that we didn't do more romantic or exciting things. I'd probably say that it's because it's something he never did with any other woman. I had a Houdini thing. I like the whole idea of making magic.

I have a good friend who always remembers the things I say to her. I don't remember the things I say to her, but she'll say, "Remember when I asked you… and you said…?" No! But it's helped her, she tells me. Of all the articles I've written, her favorite was one that never got published. She frequently mentions it.

Over the years, I've taken my son to Europe and North America and tried to both literally and figuratively give him the world. What he remembers with great fondness, however, is how I used to do foreign-country day once a month. It was a fun activity where we chose a country and I'd teach him a few words in the native language, we'd eat the food of the said country, maybe dress up, I'd give him a history quiz and we'd make believe we were doing something touristy in that country.

The things that make us memorable to our friends and family, that make an impression, that leave their imprint, are the little things. It's not the major achievements, the *simchahs* we organize, the awards we get, the showy stuff we do, the major trips we take, even the generous acts of kindness (though these are important, too). What differentiates us from other people in the hearts and minds of our family, friends, neighbors, and colleagues are the little gestures, the encouraging words, the cute shtick, the almost indiscernible moments that light up people's lives. Like a small jug of oil meant only to last a few hours, it brings light that lasts and is remembered for generations.

I know, too, that my greatest appreciation of my friends came at moments they don't even remember but that made a big difference to my life.

It's these seemingly minor interactions we have with one another that are most lasting. Not the downpour, but the rain shower. Not the neon, but the glow of a small, constant flame. A little light that chases the darkness away.

Just Ask

We want to do a lot of stuff; we're not in great shape. We didn't get a good night's sleep. We're a little depressed. Coffee solves all these problems in one delightful little cup.
JERRY SEINFELD

When in a hundred and twenty years we really start to live (at least metaphysically), Hashem will ask us various questions about what we did and didn't do in life. One of these questions will be why we hadn't eaten certain fruits that were available to us, why we never even tasted them once. Undoubtedly, some people will answer, "I didn't know where to buy them." To which the answer might be, "Well, why didn't you ask?"

Many things are just there for the asking, but you have to ask. How many opportunities are lost to us because we don't know when, what, and whom to ask? Because we don't exert the extra ounce of effort.

As part of boosting morale in my office, the company I worked for got a coffee machine. It was very exciting! The most delicious exotic coffees at the push of a button. The coffee machine had much information written on it, all in Italian. I asked the person responsible for the machine if the coffee was kosher. He didn't know and we got into a debate about whether there should be a kosher coffee machine in the office in the first place. I guess there is nothing unusual in Israel about having a religious argument over coffee.

I decided that the most practical thing to do was to write down the name and phone number of the company, which was not in Italian, that supplied the machine, and call them to ascertain the product's *kashrut* credentials. When I called the company later in the day, I was informed that the products were from Italy and didn't have any kosher certification. I was therefore glad to learn that the person who had disagreed with me earlier had already ordered a second (kosher) coffee machine for the office.

Whether I had gotten through to my co-worker or whether it was because our general manager was religious, or because there's some law that all workers have to have the same access to food, I'll never know. But only a few days later, before I even sat down at my desk, I had a frothy, hot, sweet cup of French vanilla coffee, not only with a *hechsher* (kosher certification) but made with *chalav Yisrael* (dairy products made from milk supervised from the time of milking).

Now what would have happened had I not asked? I probably would have resented the anti-religious bias in the office, the coffee machine would have been minus one daily customer, fewer people would be drinking kosher coffee, and the worker responsible for the coffee machine would have been deprived of a mitzvah.

Hashem has given us a world of opportunities and possibilities in every area of our lives. The world is our oyster (even though we can't eat that), and its pearls are ours for the taking. All we have to do is ask.

First published in Yated Ne'eman International, whose editor of its women's section sent me a gift of vanilla tea after this article appeared, which is good because coffee actually makes me hyper.

Bully for You

Thou shalt not be a victim, thou shalt not be a perpetrator, but, above all, thou shalt not be a bystander.

PROFESSOR YEHUDA BAUER

There should absolutely be no tolerance, or excuse made, for bullying. Ever! Bullying unravels the fabric of a human being. And society puts the onus on the victim to deal with it, not the bully. Bullies are not only found in schoolyards, though that's usually their first venue of operation. The Nazis were in essence bullies, criminals are often bullies, and so are terrorists. Trying to understand the bully and reason with him does not work. Telling the victim to ignore it reinforces victimhood, and telling the object of the bullying that they are better than the bullies (which is certainly true), or that the bullies are really jealous of them (which may be true) disempowers them. Being sensitive is not a reason to suffer.

Unfortunately, the tragic consequences of bullying have still not led to an adequate solution.

I remember one incident, which stands out because it was not the usual case of bullying at school. It happened when I must have been around ten or eleven years old. I went to a Jewish day school, and on my way home, I passed a public elementary school that was letting out just as I was passing. One day, this tall black girl, came running at me from the school with her friends. I had never seen her before then. I don't remember exactly what she did – whether she pushed me or threw me down – but it was obviously a great source of entertainment for her to make me cry. I was outnumbered and she was bigger than I was. This repeated itself, and I must have complained about it at home one day, because the following day, my father hid behind a pole, while I waited on the corner for my assailant to appear. And appear she did. She did not notice my father but started her usual attack. My father emerged (he was a Holocaust survivor, an older man, and angry). He ran after her. She screamed and ran away half-laughing, half-terrified.

She never bothered me again.

Bullies only understand one language, someone bigger who refuses to be intimidated by them, and stands up to them! Children would be better off if their parents and teachers learned this lesson and so should the leaders of countries.

One Kind Word

We small people can change this big world, one smile at a time, one kind word at a time, one mitzvah at a time.
RABBI MENACHEM MENDEL SCHNEERSON, THE LUBAVITCHER REBBE

I was teaching an English course for students who were trying to pass their matriculation exams. Classes were held once a week over the course of several months. The only adult contact I had in the building was the janitor, who was supposed to make sure that the classroom was open and that I had chalk.

This janitor was the stereotypical grumpy, gloomy Gus. He was such a caricature of a grumpy old man that it would have been funny, except for the fact that I needed chalk and he had the key to the storeroom. Every week I would come and ask for the chalk, and he would growl softly at me and open the door if it was locked. I really resented being in this position every week, and I sought a solution.

At the time I was reading a self-help book on getting along with people, and with nothing to lose I decided to try one of the strategies in the book, which was to make the other person feel important, valued, and appreciated. How do you make a grumpy janitor whom you know nothing about feel important?

"You know," I said gingerly to his belligerent back, "I'll bet this school couldn't run without you. You're responsible for everything that goes on here." He turned around wide-eyed. A big smile began to split his face like a fault line in an earthquake, creating caverns of smile lines in his wrinkles. He was transformed.

"You're right," he told me, beaming. And then he began to regale me with stories of everything he did and had done at the school during his decades-long career. He told me about his life, his family; he wanted me to come home and meet the wife. He wanted to have me over for dinner, to meet the grandchildren – an offer I politely declined.

For the rest of the time I was teaching the class, not only did I have long pieces of clean chalk waiting for me on the board, but the classroom had been cleaned, the desks arranged, and Mr. Janitor – nay, School Superintendent – was waiting with a big smile and his chest, puffed out, ready to prove himself worthy of my accolades.

And while this man had been transformed right before my eyes, it was most transformational for me, because I had learned the incredible power of a kind word. Whenever I speak on the subject of the power of words, I find this story to be the most illustrative of what just one kind word can do and how famished we all are for a bit of recognition and appreciation. I don't know how much English those kids learned from me, but I know I learned a valuable lesson from one appreciative old man.

Reprinted from 1 Small Deed Can Change the World: True Stories of Everyday Encounters with Extraordinary Results, compiled by Rabbi Nachman Seltzer, edited by Miriam Lea Rosenberg and Sara Chava Mizrahi, Artscroll Shaar Press; used with permission.

Just Pray for It

The purpose of prayer is not to get us out of trouble. The purpose of trouble is to get us into prayer.

RABBI YITZCHAK HUTNER

Around the time my late ex-husband and I got engaged, we met a preacher and his wife who were visiting Israel. They were very warm and friendly, and as they lived in the Bible Belt, they invited us to visit them on our manic six-day honeymoon drive from Los Angeles to New York where my husband would be starting his internship.

We took them up on their offer and stopped by to visit their cozy cabin nestled in the woods, which was accessible only by a large truck with big wheels. In the course of the visit, our preacher friend told us how he always got things by praying for them. He needed a stove, he prayed for it. He needed a fridge, he prayed for it. And these things showed up on his doorstep, literally. While I have never underestimated the power of prayer, to my mind, appliances were always something you "paid for, not prayed for." My husband and I just assumed that his congregants had heard what he and his wife had been praying for, and bought it for them.

As we were going to live in New York and starting from scratch, providentially my husband's aunt and uncle were in the midst of selling the contents of their home and packing up to retire to Florida. We were to be the beneficiaries of their furnishings. My husband listed everything they were planning to give us, including a living room set and a desk, but, he said, there was no carpeting.

He smiled and said with a glint in his eye, "We'll just pray for it." That became the running joke as we cleared the kilometers to New York.

We arrived safe and sound to find our new furniture waiting for us to give it a home. There was a lovely living room set and there, rolled up and propped against the couch, was a large, almost new, cream-colored rug. We burst out laughing.

The power of prayer, of asking God for what you want, knowing that He is the one Who gives you everything, is the greatest power you have to get what you want. Not in the making a shopping list kind of way but in the way that a child is given a book list for school. These are the tools the child needs in order to learn at school. In order for us to succeed in the school of life we also need things - clothes, food, a refrigerator and, yes, even carpeting.

Although God knows what we need more than we do, and He doesn't need us to ask, prayer endears us and our wishes to Him and so, in the same way a parent will give a child something they ask for, as long as it's not harmful, so too will God provide for the needs and wants of His children.

Since the day that my husband and I visited our friends in the wooded mountains in the South, I have learned a lot about the power of prayer. Yet that story has always lingered at the forefront of my mind. Sometimes God guides you to the most remote places to discover the most essential and irrefragable truths.

I have not seen the country preacher and his wife since that fateful visit. I'm sure they're still praying for their daily needs, and I have come to learn to pray for mine as well. Because God has an infinite supply of whatever we need and all we need to do is just pray for it.

First appeared on Aish.com

Who Knows?

Don't judge each day by the harvest you reap but by the seeds you plant.

ROBERT LOUIS STEVENSON

In my freshman year, I attended Brandeis University, which I really enjoyed! There was a lot of musical activity on campus. They had a regular choir, and a black gospel choir, but there wasn't a Jewish choir. Seeing as, at the time, Brandeis was about seventy percent Jewish, I thought this was an oversight that needed rectifying. So I went to the Hillel Student Society and asked if I could form a Jewish choir for the next year and if they would take care of the logistics and finances. They agreed.

My next step was to contact the music department on campus and see if anyone would be interested in conducting it. I found a graduate student who seemed eager to do so. Everything was in place for the inauguration of the first Brandeis Jewish Choir the following year. Except for me. Due to financial considerations, I transferred to McGill University in Montreal, where I completed my degree.

In May of the following year, I went to visit my friends at Brandeis and noticed a poster advertising a performance (that had already been) by The Brandeis Jewish Choir. I did a double take, then contacted the conductor I had found and learned that he and Hillel had gone ahead with the choir in my absence. While I was thrilled about this development, I was a bit disappointed that no one had bothered to tell me about it and I had found out "by chance."

I don't know the fate of the choir in subsequent years, but an Internet search revealed to me there were now several Jewish choirs and music groups on campus. Did I set a precedent? Who knows?

A few years ago, I spoke to a woman who told me that she and a group of women had undertaken to learn a book on *shemirat halashon* (guarding one's speech) for the merit of a friend of theirs who was undergoing treatments for cancer. The book they had chosen was *Finding the Right Words*, written by me. Each lady had procured a copy of the book and when they made a *siyum* (a celebration for having finished learning the book), they also had a *seudat hodayah* to celebrate the woman being, *baruch Hashem*, cancer-free. I was honored and humbled by the fact that they had chosen my book for this mitzvah. Again, I found out about this after the fact.

A couple of years ago, on my last visit to Toronto, I was staying with a close friend. She had been my roommate in an apartment in the Student Ghetto near McGill. Another friend came to visit us and we reminisced.

While we were tripping down memory lane, he mentioned an episode where I had apparently lectured someone on the street (I did this even before I was religious). I had absolutely no recollection of the incident (although it sounded like something I would do) and even now, I can't even recall what he had told me about it. Generally speaking, I have a very good memory but for the life of me, I couldn't remember it although it had obviously made an impression on him.

When we recall our deeds each year, before Rosh Hashanah, there are many that we don't remember, most whose ramifications we don't know about, and others that take on a life of their own after we have brought them into the world. This is true for good and for bad. We tend to minimize our influence because there's no way we can possibly imagine how far it extends. Like an iceberg, we only see about ten percent of how our lives play out. And we will be truly (and hopefully pleasantly) surprised when, at our Day of Judgment, we see our impact on the world and go, "Wow! Did I really do all that?!"

Our actions, our words, even our thoughts resound through eternity, touching the lives of so many countless others. Our potential is infinite and the knowledge of our impact is to a large extent hidden from us. We can leave, in the rather limited time we are here, a completely limitless impression on the world, influencing it indefinitely, infinitely, and for all eternity, with every action at any given moment.

That's both a great achievement and a heavy responsibility. Let us understand this, embrace it and continue to shine our light, which travels great distances to destinations unforeseen.

First appeared in The Jewish Press

Postscript: My talented cousin, Shayna Hunt, was talking to me about a family matter and she mentioned, as an aside, that when her married daughter had been in school, her teacher had read one of my articles from The Jewish Press to the class and her daughter had said, "That's my cousin!" Only she never told me about it and I never knew till then.

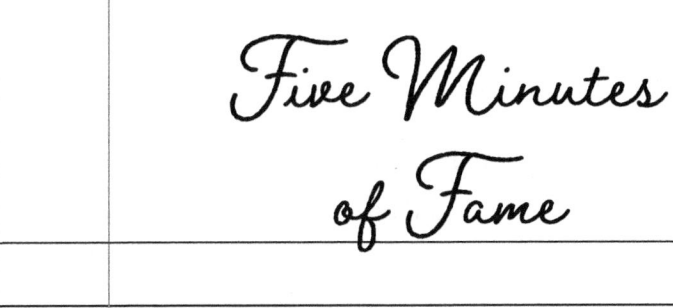

Five Minutes of Fame

There are two ways of spreading light: to be the candle or the mirror that reflects it.

EDITH WHARTON

As a writer, I send messages of inspiration out into the world, hoping to... um... inspire. But I find that I am at a disadvantage because I don't know exactly how far my message gets. Occasionally, I get feedback and when it's positive it's very nice, but I and my audience, for the most part, are and remain strangers to one another. The impact of my words is a fading echo that resonates in distant corridors. Nice metaphor, yes?

There is, however, one result that I have found is worth its weight in feedback, with an impact that resounds clearly in the chambers of the hearts of those I touch. I am speaking about the subjects of whom I write. Since much of my writing is about other people, they feature prominently in my stories. Some of them are people I am close to, others are casual acquaintances, still others are passing ships. When I write about someone and how they have made an impression on me in some way, I always try to give them a copy of the article (or the link) when it's published. The reaction I get when I do this is gratifying. People crave recognition, endorsement, acknowledgment, validation, appreciation and, in mentioning them, in giving them their five minutes in the spotlight, even sometimes anonymously, they feel important, valued, cared about, and honored.

I had a very special illustration of this once. I had written an article about how I appreciated the time and attention a colleague at work had given me (holding all calls and telling anyone who knocked, that he was in a meeting), even though I was just trying to clarify something on my salary slip. When the article was published, I cut it out and brought it to him. He sat smiling, beaming as I translated. He asked if I could bring him the whole paper. I did. I said he could now paste the article back (I was kidding). He said he would (he wasn't kidding). He told people at work about the article. A woman who never spoke to me told me she had seen my article. The man told me that he usually doesn't get this kind of appreciation at his job.

When I write about other people, and they see it in black and white, it is evidence for them that they matter, that their input counts, that they are making a positive difference in the lives of others. And when I, as a writer, illustrate this point for them by publicizing their contribution for others to see, I (and all writers) am doing something more important than inspiring or entertaining my reading audience; I am validating the significance of another human being, feeding his soul.

Though I will, at times, with God's help, achieve my goal of inspiring others and changing the world by setting off ripples in its streams, much of what I write about will be forgotten like... yesterday's newspaper. However, those whom I have acclaimed in my articles and stories will not soon forget me, and I know that, at least in their lives, by paying tribute to them, I will have made a difference.

First published in The Jewish Tribune UK

Bearing the Guilt

The worst guilt is to accept an unearned guilt.

AYN RAND

Sixty-four years ago, Rachel and her friend Miri (not their real names) went on a three-day trip down south to Masada, Ein Gedi, and Wadi David with their Bnei Akiva youth group. Being Bais Yaakov girls, they separated themselves a bit from the group (with permission) during certain activities.

While they were in Wadi David, having hiked a bit to take some pictures, they witnessed an IDF Piper plane crash in the Wadi, killing two soldiers. This is traumatic for any seventeen-year-old girl to witness, but when they heard that the soldiers had been looking for two people who had gone missing, since Miri and Leah had not been with the other girls, Miri was sure that it was them that the soldiers had been looking for, and her fault they were dead. This was further compounded by the fact that one of the pilots who died turned out to be newly married to one of Miri's friends. She felt she had not only been responsible for the death of the soldiers but for ruining her friend's life. Even though it was explained to them that that wasn't the case, Miri sank into depression, and although she eventually recovered, everyone knows never to speak to her of the incident.

While my friend was telling the story, her son said that he had looked up articles on the accident and had confirmed that the pilots hadn't been looking for them at all, they had been looking for a man and a woman who had disappeared while hiking in the area and it later turned out they had been killed by Bedouins. The plane was simply in the same area, and the crash had been an accident. The only people who might have been indirectly responsible for the soldiers' deaths were the Bedouins who killed the couple.

Miri has been carrying around guilt for the accident — something she had zero responsibility for — for over sixty years. She had misinterpreted the situation and blamed herself needlessly, enduring enormous pain.

This is an important lesson. While I'm not suggesting that we relinquish responsibility for things that we should take responsibility for, it happens many times that we feel guilty about something that really wasn't our fault because we mistakenly remembered, understood, or interpreted the situation. Usually, for any situation, good or bad, witnessed or experienced by many people, there were as many versions of the story as there are people telling it, each a different part of the reality, and sometimes divorced from it altogether.

Life is too complex and complicated to attribute a simple cause and effect to any occurrence. So many elements come into play that it's difficult to come to any simple conclusion about how any event transpires. That's why God tells us that we are not responsible for how things turn out (that's His purview). We are responsible for our intentions and for our actions but not for their unforeseeable consequences. There is a reason He is called the Master of the Universe Whose job it is to run it. We are woefully ill-equipped to do so most of the time because each of our actions, premeditated or not, sets off a chain reaction reverberating indefinitely into the future and affecting things we have no control over.

So while we need to be mindful, responsible, and careful, and try to visualize the results of our actions and where appropriate atone for them, apologize for them, and take upon ourselves never to repeat them, we should not bear more guilt than we can or should carry.

May all our actions be for the ultimate good.

First published in The Jewish Press

Coming Home

There is one place in the world to which you do not escape, nor do you immigrate, you come home — The Land of Israel.

HANNAH SZENES

Do you know that as you get off the plane at Ben Gurion Airport, there's a mezuzah on the door as you enter the terminal from the removable stairs? I never noticed it before, but I noticed it this past January as I came back from a two-week trip to North America, the first one I'd taken in thirteen years. It was a sight for sore eyes.

And then those eyes burst into tears when I saw my son waiting for me in the arrivals lounge, you know by the fountain as you exit into the main terminal? It was the first time I had traveled abroad without him in the twenty-three-and-a-half years since he'd been born. That probably added to my homesickness, although even when I'm home, two weeks can go by without my seeing him; however, that usually doesn't entail synchronizing our watches and a seven-hour time difference. And it's different when I'm 5,000 miles away instead of three.

I was so happy to see an Israeli soldier walking as we transferred from the airport shuttle to the regular bus.

I thought I wasn't going to get home. My flights from Florida to New York and from New York to Israel were cancelled and rescheduled due to an impending blizzard.

American Airlines rerouted me through Barcelona. When the EL AL plane was experiencing turbulence, I prayed not to die outside of Israel. I thought we were going back to Barcelona when there was a plane ahead of ours in line to land and our pilot circled back over the Mediterranean. But we finally, *baruch Hashem*, landed.

The next morning I was running for the bus. The grandfatherly bus driver told me to catch my breath, I could pay him later. He would have waited for me, he said, no need to run. Then a woman asked to turn on the heat. It was sixty degrees outside. I had just spent ten days in eighteen-below-zero Celsius temperatures (-4 Fahrenheit) in Canada.

One of the first things I did that morning was open the windows. I breathed in the holy air of Israel. I hadn't had fresh air inside in the two weeks I was away. They don't open the windows in Canada in winter or in Florida, well, ever.

I don't know why I was so anxious to come home. I had gone to celebrate my best childhood friend's wedding in Ottawa. It was her first wedding (hopefully, her last, of course). She's always been like a sister to me. I couldn't not go. And I wanted to go. I needed a vacation, seriously! It was a beautiful wedding! I saw people I hadn't seen in decades! We danced Israeli folk dances.

I hardly Israeli folk dance in Israel. Walking down the street is an Israeli folk dance.

I visited my old haunts in Montreal. That's what they were, haunted with the ghosts of past memories. My old school was up for rent, empty. I remembered everything, but it seems strangely unfamiliar, like it belonged to another lifetime. Well, it did.

I saw some squirrels traipsing through the snow. They looked as out of place as I felt.

My friend and I had our nails done before her wedding. It was a place run by Vietnamese women who had come to Canada for a better life. As we were waiting to leave, I noticed the small idols on the floor meant to bring peace and prosperity. And all the churches. There are a lot of churches in Canada. Montreal is called the City of Steeples. They were just background when I was growing up. Now they made me uncomfortable.

I bought something for my nails being sold by Israeli kids at a mall in Montreal, some kind of Dead Sea product to make some money before they return home to study. I felt it was incumbent on me to help Israeli youth. I also felt a need to speak Hebrew.

I felt like a celebrity wherever I mentioned I was in from Israel. Everyone was so excited. A young expectant mother I met at *shul* in Florida was so excited I was from Israel and going back and told me how she longed to go back there where she had been for seminary.

"So go back." I told her and anyone else who even slightly lamented not living in Israel (most Jews at least in theory).

My late ex-husband once said that when I'm out of Israel, I'm like a flower transplanted from its natural soil.

A rabbi once told me it's better to be a secular Jew in Israel than a religious Jew abroad. Maybe that's because a secular Jew in Israel is a bit of an oxymoron. Like an everyday miracle.

I encountered so much assimilation and intermarriage even among people I knew. And they just shrugged their shoulders as if it was par for the course. What can you do?

To tell the truth, I didn't actually officially make *aliyah* (immigrate to Israel), until I'd been living in Israel long enough to have to in order to continue living here. I sort of just came here and couldn't leave. A couple of times.

I so missed it! What was wrong with me? I was going back in a few days. I had lived in these places; why did I feel so disconnected? I had been in Israel thirty years already. Maybe it was finally irrevocably home. Not home in the historical sense, like when I was growing up and attending a Zionist Jewish high school. Not home, like where I lived and where my things were. But home, where my heart and soul dwell, which made being away physically painful.

When I came back to work, everyone was surprised how quickly two weeks had flown by. For me they were very, very long.

I ate all the food I couldn't get or that is hard to get in Israel — smoked meat and Cherry Blossom chocolates, Black Cherry soda and English muffins. I made a list. I ate almost everything on it. I gained only two kilos. Must have been all the running around searching for myself in places I had left behind.

I went to watch a friend teach at my old CEGEP (community college). The class could have been the United Nations. I counted about twenty different nationalities. It's not much different at an Israeli university, the one difference being that almost all of them here are Jewish.

I hardly kept up with the news in Israel while I was abroad. I tried but nobody was saying anything about the news. For days at a time. It was surreal! Not even my friend who works at the CBC (Canadian Broadcasting Corporation). The big thing on the news was the blizzard coming to New York.

It was great seeing my friends, whom, in contrast to the places, I still felt a connection to. Everyone was very gracious and hospitable. I was treated like visiting royalty. And the wedding was beautiful! The snow was lovely, like a postcard, despite the biting cold.

But I was so grateful to be coming Home. In every sense of the word.

First published in The Jewish Press

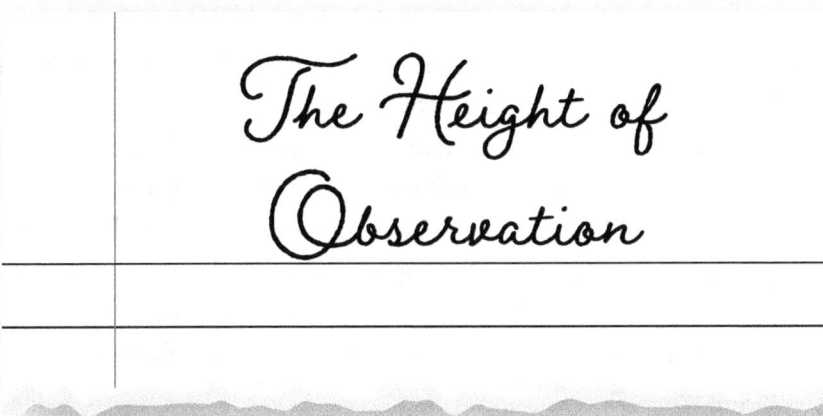

The Height of Observation

Know what is above you — a watchful eye...
                                        PIRKEI AVOT 2:1

A funny thing happened to me on the way to *shul*, when I was in my forties. Actually, it was more sad and ridiculous than funny. My son had gone on ahead and I was walking alone on the main road. A taxi stopped and asked if I wanted a lift to church. I pointed out that this was Shabbat (in Israel) and that church attendance was on Sunday, to which he replied that there are people who attend church on Saturdays (Seventh-Day Adventists). I informed him, as I kept walking, that I was on my way to *shul* (not that unusual an occurrence in Israel on Shabbat morning) and suggested he would do well to go himself (since he seemed to be more knowledgeable about Christianity than Judaism). Honestly! I then checked my appearance to see if there was anything about the way I looked that would cause the driver to mistake me (a religious Jewish woman on her way to *shul*) for a Seventh-Day Adventist on her way to church, who wants to be picked up by a taxi. I couldn't find anything, but the incident bothered me.

It was only later that the message that I was meant to receive from the incident became clear. I went to the Shabbat afternoon Tehillim group and one of the women (a real *tzaddikah*, a righteous woman) said she had seen the incident early in the morning from her balcony. She said she had been worried about the woman who the taxi driver was trying to pick up and then noticed it was me and thought to herself, "Oh, it's okay, it's Rosally; she can manage. She knows how to take care of herself."

Now this woman's balcony is a good distance from where the interchange took place, yet she had observed it well enough to see that it was me. I had no idea that anyone had been watching. And then it hit me (not the taxi, the analogy). God watches everything that happens to us — though it may seem that He's distant sometimes, He sees everything all the same. Sometimes, He'll intervene in an obvious way. Other times, He'll say, "Oh, it's okay, it's Rosally. She can manage."

Sometimes the strangest things happen to us and when, like good soul-searching servants of Hashem, we ask why, we should remember that our Master is always watching over us, waiting to see what we'll do. Often our neighbors are watching us, too. In fact, at least once a week someone mentions having seen me somewhere. With all that observation and concern, it shouldn't be too hard to feel safe and important and to do the right thing.

First appeared in The Jewish Tribune UK

A Bit of a Vice

> *The evil inclination is like the leaven in the dough. [A little makes bread good, a lot destroys it.]*
>
> TALMUD, BRACHOT 17A

My mother *a"h* used to smoke about a pack of cigarettes a day. She smoked all her adult life until she died. Even in the hospital, they let her smoke (it was less politically incorrect at the time and the cancer she had was not related to smoking). As a teenager, when I would exhort her to stop, she would respond that it was her only vice. She didn't drink, she didn't go out much, she couldn't drive (not necessarily a vice but she listed it anyway) because an operation to remove a cyst on her brain when she was pregnant with me had damaged her optic nerve and her once 20/20 vision. She did try cutting down once with a complex method involving cutting her cigarettes in thirds and smoking them through filters. But she claimed that everybody is allowed one vice and with the exception of the time she was pregnant with me, and on Yom Kippur, this was hers.

I recall that philosophy every time a well-meaning friend, naturopath, or health columnist tells me I have to stop drinking Coca-Cola. My mention of my addiction to Coke in an article once prompted a woman to write a letter to the editor vilifying its dangers and suggesting I check into a detox center. I chuckled. How bad can Coke be anyway if Rabbi Shlomo Carlebach flavored his Torah talks with it?

While I certainly don't want to encourage anyone to smoke — it's horrible and you can find better uses for your lungs — nor imbibe copious quantities of Coca-Cola (there may be a shortage), the idea of having a vice may actually help in spiritual growth.

Before anyone contemplates doing anything illegal or immoral, let me elaborate. Many rabbis have spoken of the need to give the *yetzer hara* (the evil inclination), whose job description is to try and sabotage our efforts at doing good and growing closer to God so that we can overcome him, his due. A person is a composite of an animal and a Divine being (an angel). We can go either way and that's precisely what we do, constantly vacillating back and forth, trying to inch ever higher to spiritual elevation. But when it is unable to thwart us with temptation, the *yetzer hara* appeals to our better nature and tries to make us be as devout as possible, or impossible, for us at the time. This puts us under tremendous pressure and we burn ourselves out and lose our Divine spark.

An example of this manifests itself in what is known in religious circles as "Ba'al Teshuvah Syndrome." That's when someone who discovers the joys and beauty of Judaism tries to embrace it all too fast. They take on every law, every custom, every stringency, and expect to do it perfectly. Pretty soon they've alienated their friends and family and have become overwhelmed. To emulate Shlomo Carlebach, it's like trying to down a whole bottle of Coca-Cola in one go.

There are two fundamental mistakes someone with this mindset makes. The first is the assumption that someone can ever complete the process. Hurrying spiritual growth along is like speeding through space at the speed of light (pun intended), hoping you'll get to the end of the universe faster. Becoming a spiritual person is a life's work and you don't try doing a whole life's work in one day or even one year. A person can't change a whole lifetime of behavior overnight. Another mistake is thinking that you have to be perfect. Many people give up being religious because they feel daunted by the task. They think, "Well, I can't do it all, so why bother?" But that's flawed thinking; God cherishes every mitzvah. Every mitzvah is precious to Him and to the Jewish people, and every step you take on your spiritual journey gets you closer to the goal of being who you were Divinely meant to be.

When God gave Moses the Torah, the angels protested, claiming that humans were not worthy of it. Then Moses pointed out that all the laws of the Torah pertain to gaining spiritual mastery of our desires and inclinations, eating, intimacy, greed, etc. Since angels have none of these desires, they don't need the Torah. We human beings do. God knows this and gave us the Torah so we can direct our desires toward serving Him.

Serving God is a lifetime enterprise and it takes a while to master the finer points. In the meantime, until we overcome our vices, we can direct them toward serving God as well. My mother found refraining from smoking on Yom Kippur to be much more of an affliction than abstaining from food. Her fast was more meaningful because she couldn't have the coffee or the cigarette. As for me, there's no better ambrosia for honoring the Sabbath than a tall, cold glass of Coca-Cola.

As Shlomo said, Torah's still the real thing and the Torah says to serve God with both your inclinations, good and bad. So who am I to argue?

May any good that comes from this article be for the *illui neshamah* (elevation of the soul) of Chana bat Kalman. If anyone uses this article to take up any bad habits, let it be solely on my conscience.

First published in The Jewish Press

Fanatastic

Integrity includes, but goes beyond, honesty. Honesty is . . . conforming our words to reality. Integrity is conforming reality to our words — in other words, keeping promises and fulfilling expectations. This requires an integrated character, a oneness, primarily with self but also with life.

STEPHEN COVEY

I was at a bar mitzvah where I was talking with a friend's sister. We were talking about something my son felt strongly about and then she said, "Well, you've always been a bit of a fanatic yourself." It wasn't meant as an insult and I didn't take it as one. But I have been called a fanatic in my day and it hasn't been meant kindly.

It actually doesn't bother me too much as it gives evidence of two things; the first is that I have a range of friends and acquaintances who are not like-minded, which ironically demonstrates a certain openness. The second is that I am a person of conviction, principles, loyal to my ideals, Quixotic (in a good way). After all you know where you stand with a fanatic; there's none of this wishy-washy stuff. And I'm proud of my beliefs. It took me many years to develop them and develop a positive relationship with them.

I think it's all semantics anyways. Did you ever notice that when you talk about someone who practices self-discipline or self-restraint they are a fanatic, whereas someone who overindulges or acts with no restraint is a lover of something? Compare a health-food nut with a food lover. Compare a religious fanatic with a pleasure seeker. Note a bookworm versus a sports enthusiast. It seems like people who are committed to certain ideals get bad press or bad labels.

Labels are subjective and relative. Obviously, we're likely to consider someone who is more to the right of our beliefs to be a fanatic, whereas we consider someone to the left as being not serious or committed enough. We are the yardstick by which we measure everybody else. Needless to say, someone with the same views as me is not going to consider me a fanatic no matter how extreme... um... I mean idealistic they may be. People at a protest will not call the other participants fanatics even when the police show up.

The La Leche League didn't let me become a breastfeeding consultant when I was nursing because they said I was too extreme. But La Leche is known as being extreme. I should have fit right in. It's all relative.

Do you know where the word fan came from? Yes, it came from the word fanatic! Yet somehow when it's abbreviated, it takes on a positive quality. But when it becomes popular, it loses some of its conviction.

The truth is I'm proud of being a fanatic. People know where they stand with me, and it's a lot easier to live in this topsy-turvy world when you know which side is up, when you're committed to things, when you have not only a view on a topic but a strong view on a topic. And fanatics make good friends because they're loyal. They're committed to their relationships, the way they are committed to their ideals.

Obviously, there are some goals and ideals that shouldn't be clung to. We have to stand up for the good that we believe in while so many people stand up for the bad. And the more fanatic we are in protecting the good, the better.

But, ah, I hear you saying, what about respect for someone who doesn't share your views? Live and let live, you say. There are no absolutes. Who's to say what's right and wrong. But can you? Aren't there? Can't you? Anarchy and democracy can't co-exist. Peace and violence can't co-exist. Religion and self-worship can't co-exist. Neither can fidelity and betrayal. Neither can devotion and apathy. You gotta pick one. You gotta choose a team. You need a moral compass, an ethical code to live by and be ready to die for. If you're not ready to sacrifice for your beliefs, put your money where your mouth is, even alienate some people, well then, where's your integrity? Is this the voice of fanaticism or of a person with a purpose, with a cause?

Well, I'm sure you have your own take on this. Everyone is a fanatic about something. And I don't mind if you call me one. I'd be much more insulted if you didn't.

After all, everyone needs a fan club.

Master of Our Destiny

Within one linear centimeter of your lower colon there live and work more bacteria (about 100 billion) than all humans who have ever been born. Yet many people continue to assert that it is we who are in charge of the world.

NEIL DEGRASSE TYSON

Although it says very clearly numerous times in the High Holiday liturgy that it's God who decides who shall be born and who shall die, we spend a great deal of time, energy, and worry trying to manipulate events in our favor, giving the seeming impression that we are masters of our fate.

In the summer of 2001, a family from my neighborhood decided to move to the United States because of the stress of the security situation here in Israel. They were tired of always looking over their shoulders in fear of a terrorist attack. They moved to New York. Imagine how they must have felt, only a few weeks after leaving Israel to escape terrorism, to find themselves in the middle of one of the most horrific terrorist attacks in history, especially in a city not used to dealing with it. They have since moved back.

A friend of mine married at the age of forty-one for the first time. She tried to get pregnant but experienced fertility problems. One "tactful" doctor metaphorically described it as her being a train hurtling one hundred and eighty miles per hour toward a wall. Her two failed fertility treatments seemed to prove his prognosis. Then, at forty-three, she gave birth with no medical intervention to the most precocious little girl, now in her twenties, till a hundred and twenty, whose antics over the years have been the inspiration for a couple of articles of mine.

The most incredible story is one I heard from a co-worker. Several years ago, the company we worked for was located in Bnei Brak and employees used to take their coffee break outside overlooking a side street. The following unfolded before their unbelieving eyes. A car was hurtling down the street, a bit faster than necessary. It hit a horse that was being driven across the street perpendicular to it at just that moment. The horse was thrown into the air and landed on the roof of the passenger side of the car, dying on impact and killing the passenger in the car. Imagine for a moment the person filling out the form listing the cause of death.

Like the story above illustrates, everything is from Heaven, literally.

There are books full of stories, notably those in the *Maggid* series by Rabbi Paysach J. Krohn, among others, that offer amazing stories of *hashgachah pratit* (Divine providence) where people's lives were miraculously and incredibly saved, sometimes even without their knowledge.

There's a whole book of stories telling of the miraculous rescue, Divine providence, and unfortunate deaths associated with 9/11.

People think they can control their destinies. They think if they do certain things or avoid certain things they'll be spared from death. While it's true that *hishtadlut*, both physical and spiritual, is important and does awaken Divine mercy, only God decides who will live and who will die and how. Most people do not avoid cars for fear they will be killed by a flying horse.

I was married for seven months. I had gotten pregnant right away and then had a miscarriage. I was told not to get pregnant again for a few months; in the meantime my husband and I decided to divorce, so we did our *hishtadlut* not to get pregnant. After we divorced I returned to Israel, and as soon as my health insurance was reinstated I went to the doctor who confirmed I was pregnant. *Baruch Hashem*! It didn't matter that I was not "supposed" to be or was trying not to be or that a doctor in New York had told me I wasn't when I went to see him about some pain I was having.

Fast-forward thirteen years and my ex-husband came from California for the bar mitzvah of our son. As probably is true in other parts of the world, a bar mitzvah in Israel is more like a *sheva brachot* (marriage feast), with the celebrations spreading over the greater part of the week. My ex-husband decided to eschew the celebration at the Kotel (the Western Wall) because he was afraid of being in Jerusalem with its periodic terrorist attacks, and he joined the festivities a couple of days later.

A year and a half later, he died of a heart attack in his apartment, in a California suburb that has never seen a terrorist.

When I was eleven years old, I remember playing a game of *machanayim* (a form of dodge ball) in camp. I was very skinny and agile at eleven, but athletic prowess has never been my forte. I remember I was the last one on the team and no matter how they tried, the other team couldn't touch me with the ball. We tend to live our lives like we're playing *machanayim* with God. If we're agile enough and quick enough and clever enough, we can escape our fate by outmaneuvering Him. But that's not how it works. We can take every precaution in the world, but ultimately our destiny is in God's hands. And the converse is also true; doctors don't decide who will be born. I have another friend who was told by doctors that she should terminate her first pregnancy and that they would have to perform a hysterectomy because of myomas. A private doctor gave her hope and that child is now a beautiful young woman. Although she suffered several subsequent miscarriages, my friend has, *baruch Hashem*, five children (the last two twins).

We are sometimes aware of Divine providence, and we recognize and acknowledge God's orchestration of our lives when we "catch a bus" or "have a providential meeting" or something happens just when we need it to, but ironically, in the most life-altering events of our lives, we feel we hold the key to our destiny.

A friend told me a story about a mother who, during the Six-Day War, moved heaven and earth to arrange for her only son, who usually served in a combat unit, to serve in a relatively safe position with the Home Front Command as a border guard in a non-combat zone. The regiment that her son would have belonged to parachuted into Sharm Al-Sheikh. Not a shot was fired. Everyone returned home safely and unharmed. Her son,

Rachmana litzlan (may God have mercy) was shot on guard duty when Jordan joined the war at Egypt's behest. Now it's not that if the mother had not interfered, her child would have lived. It wasn't that she caused his death, God forbid; it was that she couldn't prevent it.

We definitely need to do our *hishtadlut*. Guarding our lives is a mitzvah from the Torah. We need to pray for our own safety and good health and that of our families, and to be blessed with children. We need to do whatever we can to protect ourselves and prolong our lives.

But in our long, miraculous history as a nation, through war, terrorism, and inquisition, from Amalek to Bin Laden, from the prayers of Sarah *Imeinu* (our matriarch) to the prayers of Sarah in Bnei Brak longing to be a mother, from miracle to miracle, from salvation to salvation, we must always be cognizant of the fact that the Master of the Universe is also the Master of our destinies.

May God bless our efforts to come closer to Him. May our prayers be answered for the good, and may we all be blessed with health and happiness, peace and prosperity, wisdom and success, love and *naches* (pride and joy), always!

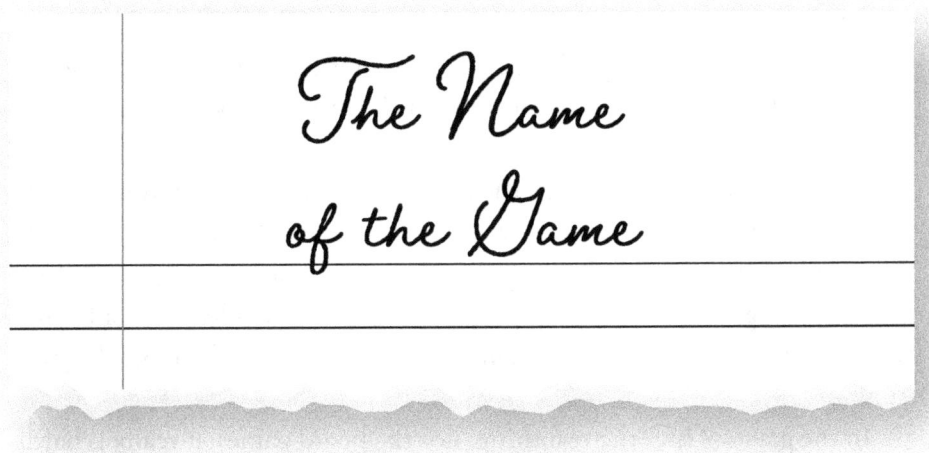

The Name of the Game

> *One does not have to play well. Just play.*
> —RABBI SHLOMO CARLEBACH

I was playing Scrabble one evening with a group of articulate women. One of the women, Joyce, an older lady who had invited me to play, is very aristocratic, aside from the upper-class British accent. If you intended to go meet the Queen and needed some lessons in nobility, I would send you to her. She's also very good-natured and fun and, well, good at Scrabble.

I happen to love Scrabble, but I don't have patience to sit and figure out all the possible letter permutations. So though my vocabulary is rich (except for all those obscure words that get you seventy points in Scrabble), my strategy is poor.

We began to play and I put down a word and she suggested, ever so nicely, I place the word down on the board another way so that I get double points.

"You're not supposed to help me," I told her.

With a dignified wave she said, "But see, if you know these little tricks, you can get many more points."

A few turns later, she chose to put down a word of lesser value, so that we could open up the board and it would be a more interesting game.

"I don't think you understand the concept of the game," I said lightly. "You're supposed to try to win." She smiled a winning smile.

In the end she did win, but she was very gracious and made me feel that I had played very well and that the difference in our scores wasn't that significant. It was. Well, since she had put down one of those seven-letter words and got doubles on some of the letters, it would have been a miracle if I had caught up.

This lady plays very much by the rules of Scrabble, but she lives the rules of refinement. I'm very competitive and I play to win. I didn't. She spent the game teaching me how to improve, smiling at me, encouraging and complimenting my game, and striving to make the game more pleasant for both of us. So we both won because, somehow, I didn't feel like I had lost the game at all.

In the game of life (the real thing, not the board game), it really is hardly a question of whether you win or lose but how you play the game. In fact, *how* you play the game actually ultimately determines whether you win or lose. It's all process. And if we focus on refining the process by being gallant and kind, generous and encouraging, instead of competitive, self-absorbed, and aggressive, then we actually all win.

So let's all play nice.

First appeared in Yated Ne'eman International
L'illui nishmat Yetta Joyce Rosemann

Drawing Closer

All Jews are guarantors for one another.

TALMUD, SHEVUOT 29A

In 1991, after the Gulf War, being pregnant and unemployed, I volunteered occasionally at the AACI (Association of Americans and Canadians in Israel), which, at the time, was located on a narrow street in South Tel Aviv. I would eat at a small, homey kosher establishment run by an older man who was obviously a Chabadnik. There was a secular school across the street, and children would run into the restaurant and the man would give them a coin and ask them if they wanted Mashiach. They answered yes and deposited the coin in a *tzedakah* box for which they were rewarded with a candy or lollipop. The kids were well-trained and very happy to contribute to bringing Mashiach.

The proprietor would do this with adults as well (though I don't remember if he dispensed candy). He asked me if I wanted Mashiach and, being certain that I was carrying him inside me, I smiled and answered in the affirmative.

There are many *kiruv* agencies (agencies that help teach about Judaism and help people become mitzvah observant), acting from many angles to bring Klal Yisrael (the people of Israel) closer to their Father in Heaven and Mashiach closer to Klal Yisrael, but I'm not sure any of their methods is more effective than that of the restaurant owner with the big white beard who made secular children believe that there was nothing sweeter than bringing Mashiach.

Fast-forward thirty years. My son has not yet been revealed as Mashiach but he does teach children Torah, is studying for the rabbinate, and works with Tzohar, one of the aforementioned *kiruv* agencies. My son also has other interests. One of them is acting (it's in the genes), and he was offered the chance to be in a commercial sponsored by the Ministry of Health to encourage people to be vaccinated against COVID. He was to represent the religious demographic.

He was ambivalent about taking the role (what if his students saw him? What if this commercial endangered his future rabbinical career?) But the pay was very good and it was for a good cause and he was assured his religiosity would be respected, so he did it. And he came home full of stories. *Kiruv* stories.

The secular director had intervened at one point in the staging to point out that my son could not stand between two women. The make-up lady told him she came from a religious family in Ramat Beit Shemesh and started discussing *Tanya* with him. The main actor in the video called him the Lubavitcher Rebbe, and the assistant stage director mumbled to herself that he represented people living in Yehuda v'Shomron (Judah and Samaria). One actor borrowed his *kippah* to make a blessing on the kosher food supplied to the cast and crew, and then offered to team up with him to do a standup show to help bridge the secular-religious divide.

Now my son might be worried about his religious credibility, but I thought this whole thing sounded like a big *kiddush Hashem*. Interestingly, in Israel a lot of theater and television personalities become religious during their career and subsequently use those media to do *kiruv*.

Kiruv isn't something only for the rabbis to do, or for the professionals who've been trained in the art. It's something we all can do, whatever we do, all the time, whatever niche we happen to be in, by being warm, sincere, pleasant, and committed.

It's as easy as offering candy to a child.

First appeared in The Jewish Press

The King's Emissary

> Blessed are You, Hashem, our God, King of the universe, Who fashioned man with wisdom... Who heals all flesh and acts wondrously.
>
> MORNING BLESSINGS

In the early 1900s many Jews left Russia, but before making *aliyah* to Israel, they spent a decade or two in Egypt. My mother's family was among them and she was born in Alexandria in 1924. It took my mother *a"h* many tries before I understood, explaining to me why she wasn't Sephardic even though she was born in Egypt and had dark hair and olive skin. When my mother was nine years old, her family moved to Tel Aviv.

From the ages of two to four years old, she would tell me, she was very sick and had typhus, meningitis, and other illnesses that threatened her young life. She became so ill that the doctors had put her in an area designated for terminally ill patients. The story goes (as she heard it from my grandmother *a"h*) that the king's doctor (the king at the time would have been King Fuad I) was visiting the hospital. He saw my mother and asked what was wrong with her. The attending physician told him and he examined my mother. After concluding the examination, he stood up and slapped the attending doctor on the face. "You idiot," he told him. "You're treating her for the wrong thing." The treatment for my mother was quickly amended and she survived, *baruch Hashem*.

A few years later, the hospital doctor ran into my grandmother walking with my mother. "Ah, I see you had another daughter," he said to her. "No," my grandmother answered, "this is the same girl you put to die in the terminal ward."

My mother often recounted this story because of the incredible *hashgachah pratit*. If the king's physician hadn't visited the hospital when he did, neither my mother nor I, for that matter, would have lived to tell the tale. He was both the king's and the King's emissary.

When my mother was pregnant with me, the doctors discovered a cyst on her brain. The cyst was removed and again, *baruch Hashem*, she survived. This time, the doctors chalked up the early detection and intervention to the fact that she was pregnant. Of course, it was another case of *hashgachah pratit*.

During the brain surgery, they severed my mother's visual and olfactory nerves. She was able to see but was left colorblind and nearsighted in a way that glasses couldn't correct, and she lost her sense of smell. Oddly, although she often asked for my help in seeing and smelling things, she never complained about it. She made adjustments like never changing her cologne. Maybe because she realized that the trade-off was the gift of life.

My mother died at fifty-seven, when I was almost twenty-one years old. Everyone at the *shiva* talked about how young she was to die, and she was. But I also knew that she had been regifted life on more than one occasion and so she had actually lived to a ripe old age.

L'illui nishmat Chana bat Kalman.

First appeared in The Jewish Press
Reprinted in Eternally Grateful

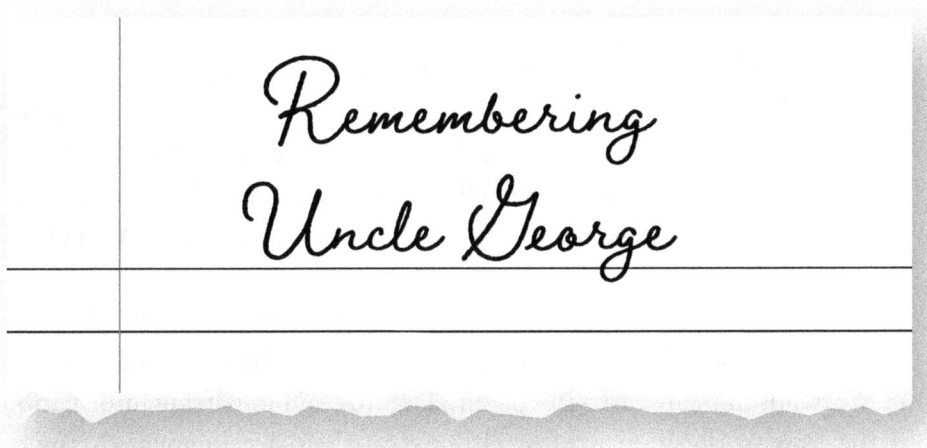

School bus drivers go the extra mile.

As the scent of autumn entices us with promise of cooler weather, and children are packing up to go back to school, I had a nostalgic moment. I remembered Uncle George.

Uncle George was a jolly middle-aged French Canadian with a mustache, a cigar dangling perpetually from his lips, and a ready smile. He was my bus driver when I went to nursery school. Although nursery school was a seven-minute walk from my house, Uncle George took us on what seemed like a very long and circuitous route in his olive-green van smelling of cigar smoke. This was before the days when that would not have been allowed and seatbelts would have been compulsory. But I liked Uncle George and I have always liked the smell of cigars because I associate it with him. He used to sing to me a French song about how he's pining for a girl named Rosalie. Believe me, there aren't a lot of songs with that name.

Leaving home was rather traumatic for me and I cried a lot. I remember Uncle George compassionately returning me home at least once. But his good humor and his booming voice didn't waver. And I'm sure that my foray into the world of education would have been a lot worse if not for him. This was many decades ago, so I assume Uncle George is now blowing smoke rings into clouds and singing his songs in a celestial chorus.

My primary years were sprinkled with a lot of people. I remember, for example, that my elementary school bus driver (still driving the seven minutes) used to make fun of me. I have no fond memories of him. Bus drivers, school lunch matrons, teachers, principals, Brownies and synagogue youth-group leaders, my piano teacher — all played a part in imparting knowledge and life lessons. They all left their mark to a lesser or greater extent and, consciously or unconsciously, helped mold me into whom I have become.

When we send the kids off to school for another year of scholastic trammels and adventurous erudition, we're putting their hearts and minds in the hands of many surrogate parental figures, and imparting information is the least of the influence they'll have on their development. Many of them will nurture, some will have only a passing effect, and some will cause damage. Irrevocable damage. It is incumbent upon us to make sure that our children are surrounded by loving and encouraging people who will smooth the path to our children's independence and pave it with happy memories and positive experiences.

Over the years, I've run into my nursery school teacher. She was also very nice and I eventually stopped crying about going there. I don't remember seeing Uncle George after nursery school. But if I close my eyes, I can still hear him singing my name and I almost get a whiff of his ever-present cigar.

Leah's Luncheon

Friendship is a sheltering tree.
SAMUEL TAYLOR COLERIDGE

When my best friend, Leah, finally got married at age fifty-four, there was no way I was going to miss the wedding. I arrived from Israel in Ottawa, in January, in the midst of, to my delight, a typical Canadian snowstorm.

The prenuptial activities proceeded as planned as we prepared for Shabbat. A couple of Leah's friends had planned a festive luncheon for the *Shabbat Kallah* that lacked only one thing, the *kallah* (bride). The combination of pre-wedding jitters and vernal temperatures conspired together so that the bride stayed home with her cold and her mother stayed with her while we celebrated without them.

At some point, when we were all sitting together, people started telling Leah stories; stories about how kind she is, how considerate, how loving, how thoughtful, how she worries about her friends and always tries to help them.

Now, at this point, I had known Leah for half a century and she had been my best friend and soul sister for most of it. But, like the sun in the sky and flowers in the path, I had just grown accustomed to it.

Listening to the stories, I was overwhelmed by the gift of such a best friend —and I'm sure there are others who claim her as their best friend, too — and burst into tears.

Leah, as mentioned before, was not part of this banquet honoring her, and it certainly would have made her blush in her self-effacing way, but it made me appreciate, as never before, why she had been my friend for fifty years and made me make a resolution never to take her for granted again.

The wedding was beautiful and her husband is one lucky guy!

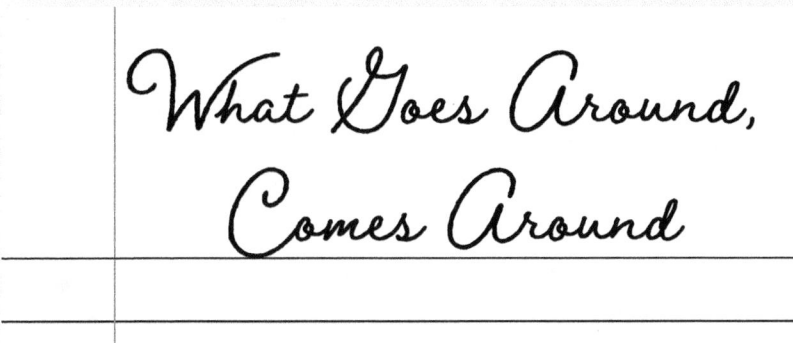

What Goes Around, Comes Around

It's good to have money and the things that money can buy, but it's good, too, to check up once in a while and make sure that you haven't lost the things that money can't buy.

GEORGE H. LORIMER

I love old things, used things that once belonged to other people, things with personal and cultural history. Especially things that are cheap. In North America this penchant can be satisfied on any Sunday by visiting yard sales, estate sales, garage sales, street fairs, antique shops, thrift shops, collectible shops, collectible fairs — all a paradise for good deals, bargains, finds, and lots of fun.

In Israel, we have *gemachs*, or bazaars, with the added spiritual dimension of raising money for a good cause and the practical dimension of helping people get rid of stuff they no longer wish to possess. No, we won't call it junk. If nothing more, it once had some sentimental value.

In my neighborhood, there are a couple of righteous women who organize a bazaar every couple of months to provide food for needy families and for households in the neighborhood to deposit their unwanted goods and purchase someone else's unwanted goods, which will, eventually, be unwanted again and re-donated to the bazaar.

As I had just moved to a smaller apartment and it was just before Pesach, I donated bags of odds and ends in a variety of subgroups: toys (with my then eight-year-old son's permission, of course), clothes, household goods, and miscellaneous paraphernalia.

A week before Pesach, the ladies held their bazaar and I went along with my son to bargain hunt. I left with a whole new wardrobe of "fresh" clothes, which totaled twenty shekels. My son picked up a cheap set of rackets, which only cost two shekels. Even though I was sure he had the same set at home, I let him have them so that he would leave the bazaar feeling the satisfaction of having found something he wanted and paid for it with money that went to a good cause. Especially since he *had* donated so much of his own stuff to begin with.

When we got home, I tried to think where my son's own set of rackets were. Then I remembered. I had donated them to the bazaar. He had actually bought back his own set of plastic tennis rackets.

There is a spiritual and universal rule that whatever good you do in the world comes back to you, sooner or later, one way or another. I never imagined the rule could manifest so literally and so quickly.

First appeared in Yated Ne'eman International

Welcome to Rosality

If things do not go the way you wish them to be, you should then wish them to be the way they are in reality.
RABBI MORDECHAI OF LECHOVITZ

My late ex-husband used to say that I live in Rosality (as opposed to Reality) I took it it as a compliment. Like when my father used to call me a gypsy. Anyway, I thought that would actually be a good name for a wish-fulfillment business. So I began advertising a service called *Rosality* that offered creative and unique ideas for gifts and celebrations.

I got my first client — a woman who wanted a family of olive-wood kangaroos for a bat mitzvah present. I hopped into action and contacted Moshav Mevo Modi'in, which organizes an annual Sukkot crafts fair. They told me about an olive-wood factory in Mea Shearim but they didn't have the number. Neither did Information. A few phone calls later, in a fit of inspiration, I called Egged tours in Jerusalem and asked them if they knew how to get in touch with such a place. The man who answered the phone didn't, but when I told him where it was and why I needed them, he said he'd drive there and personally get the number for me just for the *chesed* of it. I was impressed, especially when he did it twice because the first time he tried, it was closed. I finally got in touch with the boss of the olive-wood factory who said, yes, it could be done in a week, exactly two days before my client would be leaving for abroad for the above-mentioned bat mitzvah. I was feeling very proud of myself for having facilitated this unique present and celebrated my success by telling anyone who'd listen about it.

I called the factory every couple of days to check on how the work was progressing and was assured and reassured that everything would be fine. On the due date, I was told that the next day my client would have the pocketed kangaroos in the pockets of her luggage. The next day came and went.

The following day (the eve of departure), I called up the factory, again, and was informed that the kangaroos had blown up.

"What?!"

Apparently they were put in the freezer and kangaroos are tropical marsupials or something of the sort and the wooden kangaroos blew up.

I was disappointed, my client was disappointed, and the factory manager was disappointed.

Rosality and reality all depend on Divine providence and either can only be altered or sustained or translated one into the other if God so wills it. And apparently, in this case, He didn't.

In a related story, I was traveling to Netanya to visit a friend around the same time, and I took with me a suitcase of clothes my son had outgrown for her son to grow into.

As I was waiting for the bus, a tour bus pulled up and some people got on it. "Wait!" I jumped up. "Someone forgot their suitcase." A woman at the front of the bus claimed it for whoever had forgotten it. The bus sped off and I felt good about having done a good deed. Then I realized I had given her the baby clothes in the brand new suitcase my son's grandmother had just given him.

Apparently their destined destination was not my friend in Netanya.

Everything has an address. We're just messengers.

This appeared in some newspaper, but I can't remember where.

Day of Judgment

What does Hashem require of you but to do justice, to love kindness, and to walk humbly with your God?

MICAH 6:8

We have often had described to us the scene we will be faced with when our Day of Judgment arrives on our one-hundred-and-twenty-first birthday. I personally had never felt the full impact of what that day in court might be like until I went to an earthly court over a large sum of money that was owed to me.

Suddenly, I was called upon to respond to accusations, recall dates ad events that transpired long ago, remember what I said (and thought) on those occasions, and prove my rights to the demands that I was making.

I said *Tehillim* fervently. Not so much because of the money (although it was a million dollars), but because my destiny seemed to be at the mercy of a judge and all I could do was to plead my case. And suddenly, I understood.

I realized how it must feel when it comes to render accounts. Not only how I spent my money, but how I have spent my life. I sat there looking at my attorney who, with her blond hair, looked very much like a defending angel, at the other attorney, trying in the best interests of his client to make me look as if I had shirked my responsibilities, and at the judge, sincerely trying to be reassuring, merciful, and just to both parties. And suddenly, sitting there in helpless limbo, I was afraid because I saw a glimpse of what it might be like in The Superior Court.

If I became much more scrupulous regarding mitzvah observance and prayer before this trial, how much more did I suddenly become aware of my obligations regarding a much Higher Court, made up of defending and prosecuting angels and the Almighty Himself.

It was not hard for me to imagine that Yom Kippur would never be the same experience again.

My judgment wasn't rendered immediately. When I turned tear-filled eyes to my attorney (this case had been going on for several years already), she said to me that perhaps Heaven wanted me to achieve a higher level of sanctity. She was undoubtedly right. She was sure then the verdict would be in my favor.

I did end up winning my case but subsequently lost when the other side appealed.

I consider myself fortunate that in *Beit Din Shel Ma'alah* (the Heavenly Court), the prosecuting angel has no right of appeal.

First appeared in Yated Ne'eman International

The Secret to Happiness

There is no path to happiness; happiness is the path.

In an effort to find ultimate happiness and write a bestseller, I decided to write a book on how to achieve happiness. My working title was *500 Steps on the Path to Happiness*. I asked over fifty people to give me a list of ten things they do that make them happy. I figured I'd get a few hundred, voilà — my book would be written, and everyone would be happy. Literally.

Well, I got a great response. People who never usually answer my emails were delighted to wax philosophical about what makes them happy. It made me feel . . . happy. But then there was a little glitch in my plans. Everyone's responses fit neatly into ten very basic categories of happiness-inducing behavior. There weren't five hundred things; there were really only ten. As my friends range in age over decades, work in various professions, affiliate differently religiously, and live in many countries, they are an eclectic collection of unique individuals. Didn't matter, same list.

Okay, so now I would write a book entitled, *The Ten Steps on the Path to Happiness*. Catchy, no? I tried to expound on the theme. I got to only about thirty pages. I felt like I did in high school when we had to write one of those 3,500– to 5,000–word term papers for English Lit. I would sit there counting the ifs, ands, or buts. Funny that I became a writer when I used to agonize over term papers. Then my computer crashed and took all my documents with it into the black hole of cyberspace. I may have backed it up, but between you and me, it was like one of my term papers. But far be it from me to deprive the world of the secret to happiness even though I can't make a million dollars from it.

So, I give you the ten ingredients to happiness free (with this book) because, after all, happiness is a gift from God. To access it:

1. Commune with God

Having a relationship with God makes one feel at peace with the universe, protected, significant, real. It gives one harmony. Communing with God is easy and always accessible. Pray, say *Tehillim*, have a conversation with God, or just marvel at His universe and count your blessings. Anytime we are intimately and actively aware of God's presence, we automatically feel better about life.

2. Commune with nature

Nature comes in all shapes, colors, textures, weather conditions, and awe-inspiring panoramas. It's as close as the rose bushes and trees on your street and as vast as the oceans, mountains, and tundra. And it's all beautiful! If you're looking at pictures in National Geographic, walking your dog, or mowing the lawn, you're communing with nature. If you're watching a snowfall, walking in the rain, or riding a bike on a trail, you're communing with nature. And it's wonderful!

3. Give or receive love

Love is the critical ingredient in our lives. Rabbi Akiva tells us it's the key to being Jewish, and any psychologist will tell you it's what makes life worth living. We all have access to giving and receiving love. In fact, giving love is receiving it. Whether it's hugging a child, holding a baby, visiting a grandparent, shmoozing with a friend, smiling at a neighbor, or playing with a hamster, we have the ability to hug, cuddle, and bond with anyone anytime. Love doesn't have to be only with a close family member or a soul mate. Love is all around if it's in our hearts.

4. Help others

When we help others, we feel good. That's because doing good feels good and because when we help others we can feel grateful for all we have to share. It doesn't have to be a grand gesture like donating a hospital wing or working in a soup kitchen. It can be opening the door for someone, lending a friend a few dollars when they're short, giving a tourist directions, or helping a child with their homework. Sure, do grand gestures of philanthropy, if you can, but don't let any opportunity of doing a small kindness pass you by. It's an opportunity to feel really happy.

5. Stimulate your mind

Our minds are wondrous things. We derive great satisfaction when we stimulate them by trying to solve a problem, learning something new, studying, doing a puzzle. We get great gratification from exercising our gray cells. Look how happy all those guys in yeshiva are when they've got a *sugya* (topic) they're grappling with. They're ecstatic! Don't just sit there, invent something!

6. Exercise or pamper your body

Our bodies feel happy in two seemingly contradictory states; being stretched to the limit and being luxuriously pampered. Actually Jewish tradition seems to encourage both modes in sequence: running around working like crazy getting ready for Shabbat followed by twenty-five hours of resting and feasting; building a *sukkah* for a week followed by a week of reposing in it; cleaning the house for Pesach and then lying on some pillows drinking wine. Our bodies actually need both modes for happiness. So bend and stretch, then go for a massage.

7. Do something worthwhile

We were put on earth to accomplish. Accomplishment has a very broad definition and everyone accomplishes in different areas, in different ways, and to different degrees. A sense of accomplishment, whatever that means to you personally, provides happiness. So whether you're writing a book or a note to the teacher, designing a building or affixing a shelf, anything that can be isolated and ticked off your "To Do" list is definitely something to celebrate as "Done." And ticking things off *my* "To Do" list makes me very happy.

8. Do something creative

One of the ways in which we were designed in the image of the Creator is that we are creators ourselves. We are all creative in one way or another, and working in our areas of creativity brings us a deep sense of happiness and fulfillment. When we share our creations with others, we make a contribution to others that increases our happiness exponentially. Each of us is, or should be, aware of where our talents lie. It's in the area where we can spend hours of our time producing something during which we are blissfully unaware of how long it's taking. Whether that's writing, painting, sewing, cooking, baking, building, composing ... we were created to create. Enjoy the process.

9. Be inspired

Being inspired helps us transcend the here and now and enter the ephemeral and eternal. Some people are inspired by music, others by ideas. Some people like to read, others to listen. Learning, praying, communing with nature, and creating are all forms of being inspired. A person can be inspired by a thought they've heard or read. Whatever we end up doing with the ideas we've heard, the music we've listened to, or the feelings we've connected with, inspiration in and of itself is pleasurable.

10. Motivate others

Sometimes it's easier to get others moving than ourselves. Also, once we get ourselves moving, we want company, we want to share our enthusiasm, we want to help others reach their potential. There are groups of people who make a profession of this. They're called teachers, motivational speakers, and counselors. Of course we don't have to be those things to motivate someone. Cheering a friend on, giving a bit of support or encouragement can be enough to float someone's dream off the ground. And when we do that, we're on cloud nine.

That's it. Doing any one of the above ten things universally brings joy in its wake. Even thinking about doing those things makes us feel better. Admit it, you're feeling happier, aren't you? You're starting to smile just from thinking about walking in the woods at sunset with someone you love singing *The Colors of the Wind* while eating your favorite chocolate, which you bought from girls selling them to raise money for their school and reciting a chapter of *Tehillim*.

Now, for a dramatic ending, I looked for a quote on happiness to sum up and wrap up this article neatly. All the quotes I found made one or the other of the points above. So enough said. I'll just quote Bobby McFerrin: "Don't worry be happy!"

Now pass it on . . .

Thank you to all those who contributed to this article.

First appeared in The Jewish Press

Roughing It

In order to serve God, one needs access to the enjoyment of the beauties of nature – meadows full of flowers, majestic mountains, flowing rivers. For all these are essential to the spiritual development of even the holiest of people.

RABBI ABRAHAM BEN MAIMONIDES

My son went on a three-day camping trip with his youth group when he was eleven years old. For three days he walked from campsite to campsite, didn't have access to normal washrooms, didn't bathe, hardly slept, didn't brush his teeth. I sent a fresh bar of soap with him and he returned with it fully intact. In other words, he had a great time.

Some of the happiest times of our lives are when we're roughing it — camp, setting up house as newlyweds, or vacationing on a shoestring. When I was a university student in Montreal, I lived with a roommate in a two-room apartment in a section of downtown, near the university, affectionately called The Student Ghetto. It was very romantic and idealistic to share an apartment with my friend Farla and live as a "poor student." If you go to yeshiva or seminary, you get a similar experience. So why is this lifestyle so ideal and wonderful in specific frameworks and considered the blight of poverty in others?

There are a number of psychological explanations: it's okay when you're young; it's only for a few days, months, or years; it's a choice, not a last resort;

and when we put our mindset to it, it has different connotations. But the nitty-gritty is that if we can survive it, and even enjoy it, under one set of circumstances, we should be able to survive it (and enjoy it) under others.

Now before you give up toiletries and indoor plumbing, I'm not saying that you cannot have these things, only that you do not *have to* have them or any other "basic amenity." We tend to get used to a certain standard of living and can't imagine living any other way. A friend of mine told me about a woman who used to take three trips abroad a year and now takes only one as part of tightening her belt. For her, this is truly cutting corners, but it's a reflection of what one woman has habituated herself to. Any lifestyle, rich or poor, is first and foremost a matter of habit.

There's a story about a rich man who used to sit out in a dung heap every day with the poor, to accustom himself to it, should he ever be reduced to poverty. There are people who grew up poor and, though they came into money, still live as if they were poor. They don't need more that what they were used to.

A year earlier, I had taken my son abroad. I saved up, went into debt, pulled out all the stops, and went to Canada, the United States, and Europe (ostensibly, we were mostly visiting friends and family).

The following year, he went to (the aforementioned) overnight camp with his youth group and friends, visited *kivrei Tzaddikim* (graves of righteous people), got a *brachah* (blessing) from Rav Kanievsky, and did the local summer attractions. I asked him the rhetorical question, already knowing the answer. "You had a better time this summer with your friends than you did last year, didn't you?" He shrugged. "Just about," he answered. And if you compare the two lists, you'll notice that what was more fun and cheaper was also better for his spiritual growth.

Forgive me as I wax nostalgic again. One of my favorite summer pastimes was walking with my friend Marcy to get an ice cream as a teenager. The return trip took about an hour. One time, it was pouring rain and we frolicked in the puddles, arriving at her house drenched. That's one of my favorite summer memories, and I was also taken to Europe.

Many people know that less is often more and that many successful people, among them *gedolei hador* (Torah leaders of the generation), grew up in abject poverty. While it isn't necessary to live under the turn-of-the-century standards prevalent in Eastern Europe or the *Yishuv* (early settlements in Israel), we can lower our standards a bit and still enjoy life. Maybe even enjoy it more.

I'm not suggesting we all become homeless, but if we consider the possibility of "roughing it" on a more than once-a-year basis, and not panic about what emotional scars this may leave on our families, we may be giving them, and ourselves, an experience that money can't buy.

First appeared in Yated Ne'eman International

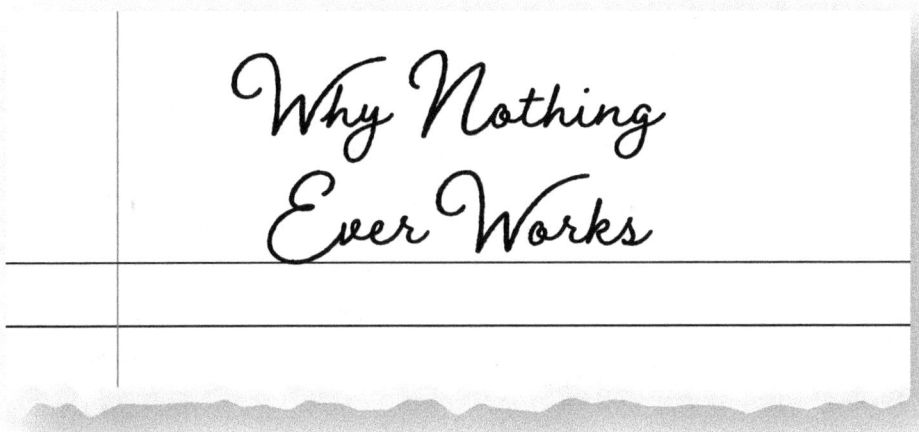

Why Nothing Ever Works

It is good to pray and dialogue with God in the field among the grass and trees. When a person prays in the field, then all the plants and animals join in the praying and help him or her, giving strength to the prayer.

RABBI NACHMAN OF BRESLOV

In 2002, I was at the Kotel when I overheard a woman and her husband discussing the question of where their daughter had disappeared to. They had gotten split up and now the woman was fretting about where her daughter was. Although she was concerned, the main complaint seemed to be that she had wanted to come to the Kotel to pray and now they were occupied with locating an eleven year old. The woman asked the rhetorical question, "Why does nothing ever work?"

I recognized this plaint from myself, and I even heard it from myself a few minutes later when I got annoyed at my son for not letting me take a picture where and when I wanted. He still wanted to pray some more and didn't want to turn his back on the Kotel, which would have been necessary had he let me take the picture in the area I wanted to.

I eventually got my picture and I'm quite certain that the woman was reunited with her daughter and got to pray. But the question remains, "Why does nothing ever work?"

Well, of course, we all know that this isn't really so and neither I nor that mother actually believe it to be. It's an expression we use when we're annoyed. The aforementioned woman was at the Kotel with her husband and three children, attesting to the fact that a lot in her life is working very nicely, *baruch Hashem*. Her husband even offered to let her go pray while he located their misplaced daughter. They were Americans, which indicated that they either were on vacation or had the good fortune to have made *aliyah*. They looked well-dressed and well-fed and, while I was exposed to their lives but briefly and superficially and am not aware of any of their challenges or difficulties, things looked to be working nicely, at least on the surface.

While I would be grateful if my only problem were getting my son to pose for a picture in accordance with my whims, things in my life, *baruch Hashem*, most of the time work in most areas, *bli ayin hara, pftoo pftoo, pftoo*.

So why do we get so panicky and whiny when things don't go the way we plan? There are many spiritual, psychological, and philosophical ways to address this topic, but I will answer simply that things that don't seem to be working to us are actually working according to a Higher plan. That distraught mother at that moment was meant to be looking for her daughter, and I at that moment was meant to be letting my son pray. Even at the Kotel, where everyone comes to do God's will and offer up prayers, even there, we are not necessarily only meant to be doing only that. When things don't work, it means that we have momentarily mixed up our job descriptions, and when they do work in sync with our limited and prosaic plans, we have to be grateful and notice.

We are on a road with many turnoffs, a path with many forks, and we often have to make detours that actually help us stay on track in order to reach our final destinations. It is not for us to question why, but what for and how.

First published in The Jewish Tribune UK

Your Own Thing

How do you tell a real diamond from a fake? A real diamond has flaws.

Everyone has their thing. You know, that issue that troubles them and others that they can't seem to change about themselves.

For example, I was spending the day with a friend as she was running errands. She needed to make some phone calls but didn't have the numbers handy. This is because she writes things on pieces of paper and then forgets where she puts them. This is easily remedied as she calls me or another friend who has the number she's looking for. But it drives her crazy that she does this and that she can't seem to stop. While I was driving around with her, a mutual friend called. Her thing is being late. She was supposed to go over to my friend's at 12:30 but said she could only come at 2:30. She arrived promptly at 3:00.

One of the errands on my friend's to-do list was getting a parking ticket cancelled. She had parked and fed the meter, but the meter hadn't worked. She had called the municipality's number, which was written on the meter, and informed them that the meter wasn't working and they told her not to worry about it. But she had gotten a ticket anyway and now was at the municipality office that dealt with parking tickets to get the ticket revoked. Another woman entered with us. She had come because she had gotten a parking ticket for five hundred shekels and told them that in Givatayim (we were in Petach Tikvah), the tickets were only two hundred. She asked if she could appeal the fine. She further asked whether she could appeal another parking ticket whose fine had gone up to one hundred and fifty shekels from one hundred because she hadn't paid it in time. The clerk typed her name into the computer and informed her that she had in fact three outstanding parking tickets. Think about this. That's two hundred shekels plus five hundred plus another hundred and fifty plus two more tickets. That's almost a thousand shekels in parking tickets! My friend and I exchanged knowing looks. I nodded in the direction of the woman. "That's her thing," I said.

Just so no one thinks I don't have my thing . . . I know where every piece of paper I write on is and I'm nearly always early for things. I don't have a car so I don't get parking tickets, but I have other issues. Like money and I'm really very sensitive and, oh yeah, Don Quixote has nothing on me.

Everyone has their thing. The reason is that we all have character traits we need to improve, and so God gives us an area in which we can work at improving them. The issue isn't the tickets or the phone numbers, the time or the money; it's the opportunity to better ourselves using this particular arena as a venue.

There's another reason for this, I think, as well. It's to teach us compassion and acceptance. Everyone has a "thing," therefore everyone should be forgiving and empathize with everyone else's "thing." It's also a way to do *chesed* by trying to help other people (only if they ask, and non-judgmentally) with their "things."

What's important is learning to recognize that we all have shortcomings and just like we want everyone else to forgive ours, we need to forgive theirs. And while we're at it, we need to forgive ourselves. Because we are, by definition, only human. And human beings have flaws and foibles.

What's also important to remember is the person who doesn't have your number can be a great friend in need, and the person who's consistently late may travel in spiritual spheres you only dream of, and the woman with the parking tickets might be giving so many people lifts to destinations they need to get to and is so easy-going and laid back that she doesn't notice the parking tickets.

So I learned that we need to love ourselves and each other, for even our imperfections and idiosyncrasies are unique and special and make us more beloved to Hashem and those around us. And loving everyone should be everybody's "thing."

A version of this article was first published in The Jewish Tribune UK

On Impact

> *I gratefully thank You... for You have returned my soul within me with compassion.*
>
> MORNING PRAYERS

Although I'm fairly accident-prone, the first time I said *Birkat Hagomel* (the blessing after surviving a dangerous experience) was when I was twenty-five and had, *baruch Hashem*, survived a car accident in which the car was totaled. I was relieved to discover that I was the most severely injured in the accident and that the damage was mainly monetary. My main fear was what my father would say when he returned from abroad. This was a talking car, but it was no longer in any state to explain things to him. It turned out all right, because he was happy I was alive, and we had insurance.

I spent three days in the hospital until my internal organs recovered from the shock. I had broken ribs and whiplash but, other than that, was in good spirits.

In fact, I was in very good spirits. According to science on the subject, endorphins surge forth during a major collision or injury to the body to help you cope with the pain and healing (or fight or flight). The residual effects of the endorphins left me in euphoria for the next couple of weeks, despite the after effects of the crash and the fact that I got tired just brushing my teeth.

I had never been so calm in my life. It was almost worth the trauma, until I discovered you get a similar feeling from nursing a baby.

That "glad to be alive" feeling, while not exactly gratitude, did mesh with those feelings and underscored my blessing at having my life spared.

We shouldn't have to experience a major accident or near-death experience to rejoice in life and tap into that euphoria. Waking up in the morning should be enough.

First published in Eternally Grateful

For Whom the Cock Crows

Write only if you cannot live without writing. Write only what you alone can write.

ELIE WIESEL

You can't sneak a sunrise past a rooster.

I had lit Shabbat candles. And the cock crowed.

We had a rooster nearby who was a bit overenthusiastic. He crowed at 5:00 a.m., when I got up. He crowed at 5:30, 6:00. He was still crowing when I left for work and was doing a repeat performance when I returned. I'd heard that roosters crow every time the light changes but this was ridiculous. I turned to my son, "That rooster never stops crowing. It's almost sunset!" A pause. "Maybe I can write a story about that."

"About a rooster crowing all the time?" he asked, quite used to my making stories out of things like pouring salt or sneezing.

"Yeah, if I can find the right metaphor."

My thirteen-year-old son went into mock philosophical mode. "Yes, the rooster crows because it's his job, his purpose in life, and because it's his purpose, he does it enthusiastically, all the time, because that's what he was made to do and we can learn from this that it's our job to study Torah and like him, we should be doing it all the time."

"That's great!" I exclaimed enthusiastically, a big smile on my face, ignoring the fact that he was joking. "That's it!"

And so I had a rooster that lived near my house. This rooster crowed all the time. Why? Because that was the job he was given by Hashem and he did it faithfully and constantly, with great alacrity, without even having read *The Path of the Just.*

We too, individually and collectively, are here to serve a purpose, serving Hashem with the unique talents He gave us. And we must do so constantly and enthusiastically with whatever talents we have been given and in whatever situation Hashem has put us.

And in so doing, we can also learn from all Hashem's creatures, for each one has a message for us.

First published in Yated Ne'eman International

Postscript: A little while after this was written, I was giving a writing workshop to a group of women. I told the above story, told them that their Divine purpose was writing, and then asked the women to stand on their chairs and crow like a rooster. And they did. I strutted around proudly for the rest of the day. Of course, they never did ask me to give another workshop.

Time Is of the Essence

Speed isn't always an advantage. Remember the snails were on the ark along with the cheetahs.

I believe that there is a correlation between how close to your due date you were born and your relationship with time. If you were born late, you are going to stay that way; if you were born on time, you will be punctual; and if you were born early, you will be early. I base my findings on informal surveys I have conducted among my friends and acquaintances, also relying on the fact that I was born two months premature and I am always, always early. Always!

Not only do I arrive at weddings I'm invited to before the bride and groom, but my perception of time is much different from that of other people. I feel that more time has gone by than actually has (like when I'm waiting), and I move faster than most people, even at my not-so-young age.

Obviously this has led to conflict with my more slower-paced travelers in this life, who are more relaxed and easy going and don't understand what difference a few minutes make.

Although I have undertaken certain strategies to remedy this time gap — bringing things for me to do when I'm waiting, telling people to meet me at an earlier time than necessary, timing how long I'm actually on call waiting, and taking deep, calming breaths, the truth is that it's rare that I find someone with the same alacrity as me (and I'm grateful when I do). I don't dance to the same rhythm as the rest of the world. It's not that I'm impatient, you see, it's that time behaves differently with me. I'm not impulsive; I'm just quick to action!

The same way we have cheetahs and sloths in the animal kingdom, people, too have their different speeds. And although sloths seem to be smiling more, as mentioned previously, I am a squirrel.

So time and time again, I beg you, please understand and try to keep up.

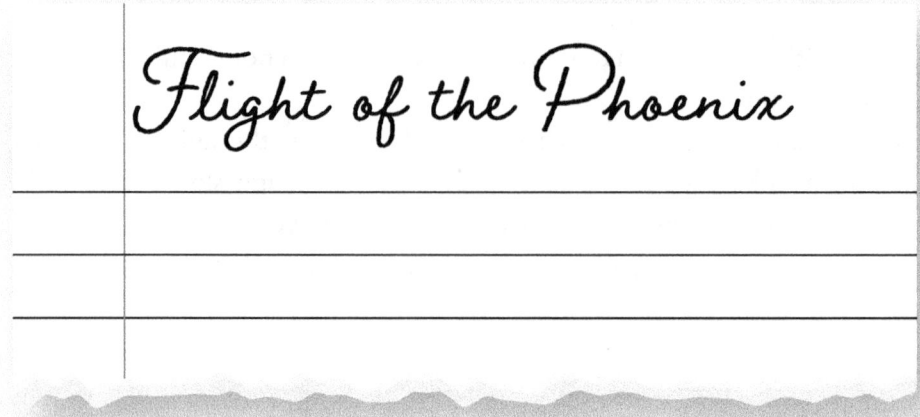

Flight of the Phoenix

In two decades I've lost a total of 789 pounds.

ERMA BOMBECK

I read about the legendary longevity of the phoenix, a creature that appears in the mythology of almost every ancient culture, as well as in Jewish sources, and has its origin in two midrashic (interpretive) traditions. One was that it refused to eat from the tree of knowledge, from which Chava (Eve) fed the other animals. The second is a blessing it received from Noah for not bothering him for food when it saw he was busy. This emphasis on the phoenix refraining from eating is a metaphor for not partaking of this world and becoming tied down to it. Perhaps this is the secret to eternal life and eventual redemption. After all, if one isn't tied to this world, one doesn't have to be purified from it through death. Or alternatively, as with the phoenix, death and rebirth can be a quick and easy process.

The phoenix is the most beautiful bird ever created or imagined (depending on your perspective on the issue), whose secret to both longevity and eternality is its refusal to make a pig of itself.

The evening after I read about the phoenix, I was invited to a Chanukah party by one of my closest friends, who also happens to be a good cook. You really have to be a mythological creature to refuse crispy latkes on Chanukah, drenched in sour cream and applesauce.

I am not, after all a mythical bird. I will have to find another way to earn eternity. Thank God, as a Jewish woman, it is easy to do so by consuming the many foods it is a mitzvah to eat. And this is one mitzvah I do *b'hiddur* (on a high level).

A version of this article appeared in Yated Ne'eman International

Par for the Course

Life is like waterfall; you have to go around the rocks.
YAAKOV ALTMAN

I'm naturally clumsy. I'm also naturally graceful. This is not a contradiction. I move very fast and so I sometimes stumble and fall, though I can master choreography. I've had two most memorable falls. The first was when I was performing at age twenty in a Gilbert and Sullivan operetta. I had to run onto the stage and up a platform, only my foot slipped and I was hanging off the platform, holding on to someone's costume. I quickly righted myself and was able to Dance a Cachucha, but my friends who were in the audience have never forgotten it.

Then there was the time, a few years later, I tripped over an ottoman in a restaurant and literally fell at the feet of the guy I was dating at the time (not the reason we broke up).

Of course the bigger they are, the harder they fall, so my falls in recent years have been a bit more painful, aggravated by the less than evenly paved streets of Israel. Luckily, in Israel, if you fall, twenty people immediately surround you to offer assistance.

This dialectic, interestingly enough, has not had a major effect on my self-confidence, either way.

We are made up of opposites and opposites attract.

Of course it wouldn't hurt for me to be more careful.

A Valuable Lesson

People rarely succeed unless they have fun in what they are doing.

DALE CARNEGIE

Scientific research tells us that there are several types of intelligence. Psychologist Howard Gardner identified the following distinct types of intelligence: Linguistic, Logical-Mathematical, Bodily-Kinesthetic, Spatial, Musical, Interpersonal, Intrapersonal, and Naturalist. There is also spiritual intelligence and many more I'm sure will be discovered before Mashiach comes and reveals the ultimate Divine intelligence.

In any event, this relatively new perception has changed the way education is viewed, and students now have a one in eight chance of being successful as opposed to the previous type of evaluation — you can do/know it or you can't/don't.

This was brought home to me when I was teaching English to a very sweet girl. For years, since we began reading, teaching her was an uphill battle. Although she was obviously intelligent, she was dreamy and had trouble concentrating, especially on reading. She would draw words out when she read and tune me out when I did. On a number of occasions, I suggested to her mother that maybe someone else should teach her. Her mother, a very nice lady, and one of my staunchest and most considerate clients, wouldn't hear of it.

Then one day, at the end of a lesson, I did a song with her. I was overcome. She had the purest, sweetest, loveliest voice, and I wanted to hear more of it. For the next lesson, I prepared another song and we spent the lesson learning it. She not only enchanted me with her singing, she learned it quickly. Suddenly, when words became lyrics, she had an uncanny reading ability and could remember what they meant.

Thus began a new learning practice. I found tapes with English songs that were appropriate, or downloaded musical accompaniment, printed out the lyrics and voilà! She enjoyed learning, I enjoyed teaching, and she learned English. When recently, her mother gently suggested that maybe we also do work from a book, I told her that we were covering all skills: reading, writing (I quiz her on occasion), speaking (singing), and listening.

I spoke to a friend of mine who's also an English teacher for reassurance. She then brought up the point of different intelligences. This girl obviously has strong musical intelligence, and when we use it to learn another subject, like English, the results speak (or sing) for themselves.

Before, this girl didn't really love to come to me, but then she became very enthusiastic about her lessons, asking to work on a particular song that she'd been singing at home, and I had to nudge her out the door when the lesson was over. That's what learning is supposed to be, an experience we relish and are eager for.

Children who are not eager to learn are probably not being taught according to their dominant intelligence. It's not that they can't master the subject; it's that it's not being transmitted through the right medium. The teaching of almost any subject can be adapted to the child's dominant intelligence, and that's the way to ensure great success. That is equally true of teachers' teaching methods.

Teachers who don't enjoy their lessons are probably not using lesson plans that tap into their students' dominant intelligence and strongest skills. Varying teaching methods in the classroom ensures that all the children, regardless of learning style, are having their needs addressed. It's also more interesting, and students can try out different styles. Also teachers who teach through their own dominant intelligence will radiate more joy to their students, who will likely enjoy the class more.

Today, when learning takes place at great speeds to fulfill curriculum requirements, this knowledge can hold the key to a child's academic career.

A Valuable Lesson

At one lesson, I told my student that I wanted her to write her own song. We would take a melody she liked and write her own lyrics for it. Her response? "Can I start at home?" Now, that was music to my ears.

First published in The Jewish Press

Into the Arena

There are no problems, only opportunities for growth.
REBBETZIN DENA WEINBERG

It took me well into middle age, but I think I figured out how life works. We are not supposed to fix our major problems. Now please bear with me.

Every one of us has a theme problem (or more than one) that has plagued us for a long time, maybe even our whole lives. For some, it's a medical problem (physical or mental); for others, an emotional problem; and others, like me, have a financial problem. Some people have difficult marriages; others can't find their *bashert* (soul mate). Some have difficult parents, others difficult children. Most of us are fighting the battle of the bulge, while some are grappling with an eating disorder.

We're all in the arena, whatever we're contending with. And here's the scoop: we're not meant to win. We may, but that's not the true objective. Our particular battlefield is the arena in which we do our spiritual *tikkun* (rectification); it is where and how we hone our characters and refine our *middot* (character traits). It is the means, not the end.

Allow me to illustrate. I have had a lot of financial ups and downs over many years. I sold some land that had been in the family for decades and used the money to be a stay-at-home, single mom. I won a million dollars in a court case, only to lose it again in an appeal. I inherited money, then had a car accident and a fire. I won a car in a raffle, which I transmuted into cash, then lost my job. I've made good investments and bad investments, borrowed money, paid it back only to have to borrow again, and finally had to graciously and humbly accept the gifts my friends gave me to help me out.

See a pattern? I never sink, *baruch Hashem*, but I never swim far. I always have what I need, but I'm always treading water. And so it hit me one day: my *tikkun* isn't to pay off my debts; it is to use my financial situation as a tool to do my true spiritual work.

The takeaway from all my financial angst has been to become more adept at patience and self-control; self-respect and respect of others, *bitachon* (trust) and gratitude, resilience and creativity; compassion and humility; optimism and resourcefulness; initiative and *emunah* (faith); appreciating friendship and recognizing Divine providence; prioritizing and lots and lots of prayer.

That's a lot of spiritual potential and work in just one sphere of life. And we've all been gifted one or more areas in which to do this work. And I mean gifted, because it's where we can mine the jewels of our destinies, celebrate victories, and acknowledge our blessings. And just for balance, we are always given other areas in which our blessings are abundant and our work easier.

Most of us use our trials and tribulations to help others in similar difficulties. Support groups and entire *chesed* organizations have sprung up from people's desire to help others with similar problems. It is as a clear as writing in the sky, as a flashing neon sign — the work isn't to solve the problem. The problem is the solution.

Each step we take in coping brings us closer to our spiritual goals, sometimes even our other objectives. Though we may never get there, it's all part of the plan. It's not the destination, it's the journey that's important. Because we're not the same person at the beginning as we are at the end. Or even in the middle.

Of course, I'm not suggesting that we stop making every effort to solve our problems. But it isn't our efforts that solve them. Hashem's salvation can come in the blink of an eye. We need to shift our focus from ridding ourselves of whatever is troubling us to dealing with it in a spiritual way, knowing that this *nisayon* (test) was designed for us to work on ourselves. Actually solving life's dilemmas is in the hands of Hashem.

I remember feeling a great sense of freedom at this discovery. Not that this frees me from my obligations, or anyone else from theirs, but realizing that this was my secondary aim, not my primary one, has given me a sense of peace, has quelled my panic. Our spiritual path is located right in the heart of the arena where we are Hashem's gladiators.

Our aim is not achievement but refinement, not accomplishment but perseverance, which will create the fertile soil in which we can flourish and perfect ourselves, the ground in which we can take root and grow and flower and bear the fruits of our toil and struggle.

And that's worth all the money in the world.

First published in Yated Ne'eman International

Mirror Image

> *When you see ill in your friend, it is your own ill that you are observing.*
>
> THE BA'AL SHEM TOV

I was at a *brit* (circumcision ceremony) and my attention was caught by one woman who, even before the actual ceremony started, had already begun to eat with relish. I looked at her disparagingly as she continued eating throughout the ceremony.

"I have to find a way to give her the benefit of the doubt," I thought. "I know! She must be diabetic." That would explain why she had to eat immediately. One of the women setting up brought drinks to her table, and my theory was invalidated when she reached for the non-dietary beverage.

After the *brit*, other people sat down, and after waiting until a couple had begun helping themselves, I, too, sat down and dug in. Being the only person of my ethnic group at this event, and knowing no one there, I self-consciously took a seat alone at an end table. Since no one knew me either, aside from the baby's parents, I basically stayed there by myself. I helped myself to the variety of salads on the table and, having eaten my fill, noticed that I had pretty much eaten all the salads on the table — all by myself.

I can't think of a truer dictum than the teaching of the Ba'al Shem Tov that what disturbs you in others is basically a character defect that you yourself have to work on at some level. Although I know I didn't reach the epicurean heights of the lady at the next table, I lacked a certain restraint in partaking of the fare.

When we are annoyed by the behavior of others, it is akin to looking in a distorted, distended mirror, the kind one finds in an amusement park's House of Mirrors. It is not really our true reflection, but it is, still, recognizably us.

Isn't that annoying?

First published in Yated Ne'eman International

The Cat's Meow

Dogs have owners, cats have staff.

Many stray cats share the Holy Land with the Jewish People. Unlike other groups who do so, they are fairly peaceful, except for the occasional caterwauling, and demand nothing of us but an occasional handout. Today, in my neighborhood, there are several women who have taken it upon themselves to cater to the cats, but it had been my practice to feed the cats that hung around the various buildings in which I have lived.

One of the cats, whom Hashem provided for through me, was a ginger cat. He didn't come around every day, which suited me fine, and he ate my leftovers, which saved me the transgression of wasting food. He disappeared for a while and upon his return, he looked the worse for wear. I tried feeding him steak; he rubbed up against my legs and turned away. A few days later, I tried hot dogs and got the same reaction. Then I met a neighbor who overheard me telling the cat that I wouldn't try to feed him as he rejects my food, and we started to discuss the cat. He said that he too had been feeding him. I told him that I had offered the best of my leftovers but he had turned up his bruised nose at them. Then we began discussing his menu. The neighbor said if I wanted to feed him, I should give him chicken with rice. So I went upstairs, where I had the week-old remains of chicken soup, took out a few pieces, and ran down again to feed him.

He lapped it up.

This brought to mind a lesson I have repeatedly heard about *chesed* that I unfortunately just as often forget. When doing *chesed*, we have to give people (and animals) what they need and want, not what we think they should have. Believe me, this cat looked in no condition to be finicky. Underweight, with cuts and bruises and some of his fur missing, he wasn't in any position to be choosing à la carte, but he knew what he wanted and what he needed and once he got it, he was purrfectly happy.

Although it's a big mitzvah to do any kind of *chesed*, true *chesed* should be from the point of view of the recipient, not the giver. Although we each have our special talents and gifts of giving, our contributions are best enjoyed when they are aimed at the person who'll utilize them best. Sometimes, we give what we think the person should receive, then judge them if they aren't happy, use what we've given them in a different way than we intended, or refuse to listen to reason or take our help. We have rules about our *chesed*, and if others don't follow them, we see them as ungrateful and unreasonable. True *chesed* is understanding the person we're trying to help and giving them what they really feel they need in the way they need it; otherwise, it's not *chesed*. On the contrary, it can end up causing them pain, putting pressure on them, and making them feel wanting in more ways than one.

I was truly happy that I had finally given my ginger friend proper nourishment. But I had nourished him in more ways than one. Because being understood is food for the soul. *Kal vachomer* (a fortiori) for a person. And he taught me a lesson about *chesed* that most people are unable to teach because of the constraints of diplomacy. David Hamelech (King David) learned a lesson about purpose from a spider. Shlomo Hamelech (King Solomon) learned about wisdom from a bee, and *l'havdil*, I learned about *chesed* from a ginger cat.

First published in The Jewish Tribune UK

> Because of Kamtza and Bar Kamtza, Jerusalem was destroyed.
>
> TALMUD, GITTIN 5

Some people hit it off right away. Their chemistry is clear from day one and they become fast and steadfast friends. Others just don't seem to hit it off. They may even rub each other the wrong way. And that's okay. There isn't a lot you can do about it. Or is there?

I belonged to a club at university that brought together a lot of diverse and interesting people. Some of us had the club in common and nothing much else. But it was a social group as much as anything and we socialized.

There was one girl who really didn't like me. This was aggravated by the fact that we both threw a party on the same night (unbeknownst to each other) and our common friends had to go to the parties in shifts. Of course, we didn't invite each other to our respective parties. When I found out, I thought it was funny. When she found out, she was not happy. Of course, neither of us did this on purpose. In retrospect, I can't understand why no one bothered to tell us so that one of us could reschedule.

Anyway, this was the state of our relationship.

One day, I was walking across campus, around lunchtime, when I found her in tears.

"Isabelle (not her real name), what happened? What's wrong?"

Between sobs, she told me that a friend from the club had promised to take her out for lunch for her birthday (which was that day) and had just reneged at the last minute. I understood how she felt. For me, birthdays are sacrosanct and I could understand her feelings of disappointment and pain.

I don't remember what I had planned or scheduled for that day, but I told her I'd be happy to go have lunch with her. I couldn't treat her because I was a student, but I would help her celebrate. So we went out to eat and somehow she was cheered up by the fact that I was company, even though I wasn't one of her favorite people.

And that's when our relationship changed. She must have appreciated my small gesture because from then on, I was her friend. In fact Isabelle and I corresponded for many years after we both left university, from various parts of the world. Our letters crossed at least half a dozen countries, as we both moved around.

It didn't take much for Isabelle to dislike me at the beginning, but then it didn't take much for her to like me in the end.

And, of course, for the many years we corresponded, we always exchanged birthday cards! I guess we had something in common after all.

Back in the Saddle

There is a fountain of youth: it is your mind, your talents, the creativity you bring to your life and the lives of the people you love. When you learn to tap this source, you will have truly defeated age.

SOPHIA LOREN

*Why were the horses so happy?
They were in a stable environment.*

I wanted to do something fun with my son to celebrate his turning thirty years old (*ad* 120). We were up north for a few days, so we went horseback riding. It was a beautiful mountain trail. The temperature was also in the 90s.

I hadn't gone riding for a long time and, truth be told, although I had ridden quite a bit in my life I had never felt completely comfortable on a horse. So I had a panic attack but then got on the horse anyway. The horses were led by a young American guy named Alex, who'd made *aliyah* and used his love and talent for horses to make a living. He held my horse with a rope the whole way, frequently turning around to give me reassurance and encouragement.

I had forgotten how much effort it was to sit on a horse. Alex kept telling me to keep my legs straight and . . . smile!

Halfway through the one-hour trail I began to relax a bit, which was good because we started to trot. Alex just kept telling me to smile, reassuring me that the horse would not go off the steep edge that we were riding along.

Baruch Hashem, I made it to the end of the trail, out of breath and gasping with thirst. My son did enjoy the horseback riding and was only disappointed that we hadn't galloped.

A few days later, my son was flying to California to visit his father's family and we drove to the airport in his new (used) car. I had to drive the car home. Again, I hadn't driven in years and was having a panic attack. He said, "Don't worry, you're a good driver... and smile!"

As I was riding the horse, whose name by the way was Dollar, I kind of came to the conclusion that my horseback riding days were over. Although Alex told me he was teaching an eighty-five-year-old woman how to ride, I felt that my heydays (or haydays) were over.

We always remember the first time we do anything. It's always a memorable milestone. But there's always the last time we do something. I mean most of us don't turn somersaults when we're twenty-five. We might not remember the last time we did it, but we will admit that our somersaulting days are over.

There is a certain wisdom and poignancy in, as "Desiderata" puts it, *gracefully surrendering the things of youth*. I think horseback riding may fall into that category. But then there are things we need to keep doing, like maybe driving, and when we do, it's best that we give ourselves words of encouragement and... smile!

If you'd like to visit the ranch, it's called Bat Ya'ar.

N.B. I spoke to my cousin, Shayna Hunt, after this incident and discovered that my paternal grandfather (her maternal great-grandfather), who died in the Holocaust, had owned a ranch in Lublin, where he raised horses that he sold to the King of Poland. I'd never known this before. Boy, have I fallen far from the family tree!

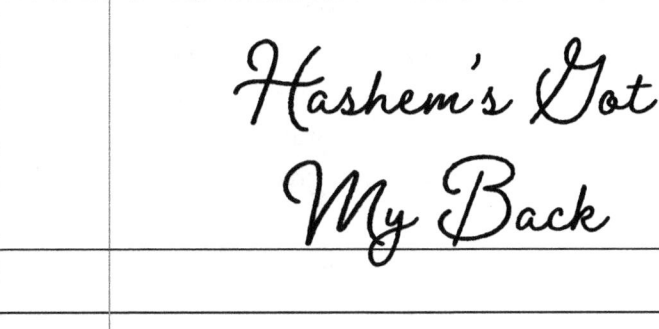

Hashem's Got My Back

87% of young people have back pain. The other 13% have no computer.

In all my efforts to cure my lower back pain — chiropractors, osteopaths, orthopedic orthotics, even an ergonomic office chair I asked my boss to buy me — I hadn't changed my mattress. But it had already celebrated its silver anniversary and was showing its age. This was brought home to me when I spent a few nights with a friend of mine in Montreal who had an Orthopedic Simmons Sleep Platinum Supreme mattress. It was like night and day (forgive the pun).

Not able to take another night on my midsummer night's dream mattress, I decided to go looking for my friend's mattress or as close as I could get within my budget. There was a Simmons store a five-minute walk from my home. Google saw me looking at it and sent me a twenty-five percent off coupon, and the woman I spoke to over the phone said I can pay for it in up to thirty-six installments. I figured even I could handle that.

As I was on my way to the store, my son sent me a picture from one of the neighborhood WhatsApp groups that someone had thrown away a perfectly new-looking mattress and suggested I go have a look. "I'm not taking a mattress from the street," I said. But when I went to the store, the payment terms were slightly different from what I had been quoted, and after finding a mattress that I thought would be suitable I wasn't able to negotiate a payment solution, which was kind of weird because you can usually almost always do that in Israel. I left the store and messaged my son, "Maybe go have a look at the mattress." Who knew if it was the right size for my bed frame? Who knew if it was even still there? He went with a measuring tape and a good friend, who always agrees to lug furniture home for me, and brought it home.

It not only was a perfect fit but looked and smelled brand new. It was a King David mattress (fit for a queen) and even had a symbol showing that it was *sha'atnez* free (doesn't include a forbidden combination of fibers), something the guy at the Simmons store couldn't tell me about the mattresses. I lay down on it. I didn't want to get up. It was perfect and free! I was overwhelmed by the *hashgachah pratit*.

I subsequently woke up, not so much with less back pain but with gratitude and the feeling that Hashem loves me. My son checked how much the mattress cost online, and I gave *ma'aser* (a tithe) to the Alyn Pediatric Orthopedic Rehabilitation Hospital.

This isn't the first time that this kind of thing has happened. But the timing was perfect and so was the illustration that when something's meant for you, it finds you. There's no need to lose any sleep over it.

First published in The Jewish Press
Reprinted in Eternally Grateful

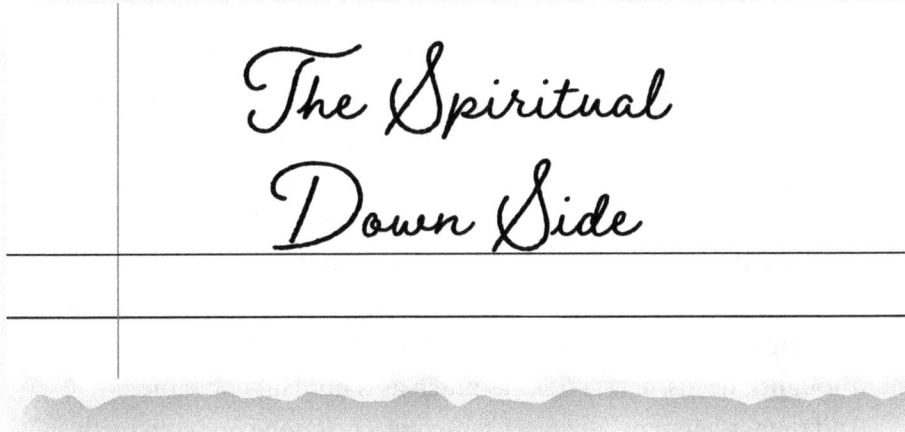

The Spiritual Down Side

> *The worst fault a person can have is to forget his intrinsic greatness as a human being.*
>
> RABBI SHLOMO OF KARLIN

My down comforter was ripping here and there, scattering feathers all over my room. So I decided I would go to a place that sold and fixed comforters. When I got there, I was told that they couldn't fix it, but they would give me a free down pillow if I were to purchase a new comforter, which was now on sale at half the price, and they would donate my old comforter to a needy family.

Okay, it sounded like a good deal: a free mitzvah, a free pillow, a new comforter. The salesgirl asked me what kind of feathers I had in my comforter. I said, I didn't know; I'm not a duck. And then I learned that there are two kinds of feathers, those with a spine and those without. I discovered the difference when I was drawn toward a comforter in one of my favorite shades of lavender. The salesgirl informed me that it was the spineless kind. It cost four times as much as the one I had opted to buy. I leaned in against it and discovered why.

It was as soft as anything I had ever touched and as I sank my face into it, I knew I could never again feel as satisfied with a regular comforter. I had experienced the softness of angel wings and one day, I would want to own a pure down comforter like that one.

And I thought what a great topic for my articles on saving money. I could talk about how we needlessly get used to luxuries and then are spoiled forever;

how we enslave ourselves to our elevated tastes by becoming addicted to the finer things; how, when we sensitize ourselves to only the best, we cannot be satisfied with anything that is not as pure and refined . . .

But then I thought better of it. There was a loftier lesson to be learned here. Every day, we work on our spiritual growth. We try to perfect our characters and are scrupulous in every aspect of our mitzvah observance and then we say, "That's it." We're done, we've gone as far as we could go and are now resting on our laurels. We've put ourselves through a sieve and purified our thoughts, deeds, and actions as much as is humanly possible.

And then it happens. We meet someone who's gone one step further. We find out about something more we could be doing. We observe someone performing an act whose level of dedication and sacrifice we aspire to, and then we realize that there's something better, purer, lighter than even a feather; something that can be cast heavenward, float higher, and transcend.

We can strive to acquire things of more value or more quality, or we can become people of greater quality. It is the spiritual as well as the physical beds we make that we sleep in, and it's up to us to decide how fine the linens we use are going to be.

Appeared in Yated Ne'eman International

The Bigger They Are

When an eighty-five pound mammal licks your tears away, and then tries to sit on your lap, it's hard to feel sad.

KRISTAN HIGGINS

I was walking in Petach Tikvah one day when I saw a couple walking a St. Bernard. I started going, "Oh! Oh! Oh!" The guy walking the dog tried to calm me down, figuring I was frightened. But I had already run toward the dog and wrapped my arms around its neck.

When I was nine-years-old, my mother brought home a St. Bernard puppy. My mother named her Aurora and she lived with us until she was twelve years old. She predeceased my mother by one month, and one of the few lies I've ever told was reassuring my mother that Aurora was fine when I went to visit her that last month.

St. Bernard dogs are gentle giants. They wouldn't hurt a fly. But anyone who came to the house had to be encouraged, coaxed, and reassured to that end. My friends slowly underwent St. Bernard exposure training before they felt comfortable coming in. After they felt comfortable, there was still the matter of Aurora slobbering and licking and her general expressions of interest and affection. I can still hear the clatter of her nails on the linoleum and her booming barks of joyful welcome.

Appearances are deceiving. We often misplace our trust one way or the other. It's important to know the nature of the beast, no matter on how many legs it stands, and the best way is when others vouch for it. Another is if it's wagging its tail in welcome.

We small people can change this big world, one smile at a time, one kind word at a time, one mitzvah at a time.
RABBI MENACHEM MENDEL SCHNEERSON, THE LUBAVITCHER REBBE

Wanted
Workers for employment. Lifetime contract — maximum 120 years. Varied work, excellent benefits, occasional bonuses. Eternal vacation pay. Must invest heart and soul. Working hours 24 hours a day, 7 days a week. Shabbat and sleep 1/60 vacation. Must be willing to work overtime. Pleasant working conditions, different locations, some close to sea, choice of climates. Transfers possible. Family-type atmosphere. Frequent promotions based on experience, willingness to learn and improve, and desire for advancement. Positions available in many different departments. Executive Director available for meetings any time; no appointment necessary.

Whether we are aware of it or not, we have all applied for and accepted the above position and now we are working at our jobs, each according to his or her specialization and goals. We, or at least, I, tend to forget occasionally that my real boss is Hashem, I'm always on the job, and whatever else I may be doing, my real work in this world is of a spiritual nature.

Sometimes, we forget to be grateful for the fringe benefits of our positions; the delicious food, the loving and supportive colleagues (our families and friends), the pleasant working conditions (sun, snow, flowers, four seasons), and the working holidays we get — Shabbat, festivals, *bein hazmanim* (intersession).

We often get depressed and gripe on our coffee breaks to the guys in the office or even to the Big Boss about something we're missing that we'd like to have. We forget that if we are missing something, it's because it's not part of our job description; it's not part of the tools of our particular trade in the universal enterprise we work for. Everybody would like something more: more wealth, more family, more love, more health; or something less: less aggravation, less responsibility, less debt, less weight. And while we certainly are permitted, and even expected, to take on new projects, strive for more benefits, and petition for what we consider better working conditions, some things are just above and beyond our call of duty and not only not required for either our job description or our job satisfaction but would actually hinder our job performance.

Everything that we need to excel at our jobs is provided. We don't need to requisition anything else. Though no one says it's easy, it's a comfort to know that we'll ultimately be rewarded for a job well done. We have good days and bad days but that needn't affect our job performance. Some of us work better under pressure. In our spiritual journey, *all in a day's work* means something else for everyone. Each contract has its own fine print.

It's important that we remember that everything is just part of the job and enjoy our work to the best of our capabilities, not only because it's been tailor-made for us, but because there isn't a nobler profession or a better job available anywhere else in the universe.

First printed in Yated Ne'eman International

About Face

For beautiful eyes, look for the good in others; for beautiful lips, speak only words of kindness; and for poise, walk with the knowledge that you are never alone.

AUDREY HEPBURN

We all face different spiritual challenges. Women often encounter these challenges in the area of modesty. On Shabbat, I personally face this challenge in the area of my face. I usually wear makeup. Okay, so I'm vain, I admit it, but didn't Hashem in His wisdom and understanding of the women He created not shower down makeup with the manna? The men picked up the bread and the women came home with blush.

Although in the desert, Friday's makeup probably stayed fresh till Sunday morning; no such luck nowadays. Even the special *melaveh malkah* lipstick that's supposed to adhere until *melaveh malkah* (a meal following Shabbat) usually doesn't last past dessert of the first *seudah* (festive meal). So on the day I host the Shabbat Queen, I look the least ready to meet royalty.

Although it's permissible to put on some types of powdered makeup, it just doesn't look the same. So on Shabbat, I don't check my makeup when I look in the mirror, as it's not there; I check to see, instead, whether the light of my *neshamah yeterah* (extra soul) is shining through. Let's face it, on Shabbos, I'm looking at the real me, with the full force of my mortality and level of spirituality staring me in the face. It's no coincidence that *Sheker hachein v'hevel hayofi* (False is grace and vain is beauty) is recited on Shabbat. Shabbat is the day for our inner beauty, our true beauty, to shine through.

Everything looks different on Shabbos — our homes, our tables, our children — so why shouldn't we? Without makeup, the *eshet chayil* can really put her best face forward.

First published in The Jewish Tribune UK

String Theory

> *You are what you do repeatedly.*
> RABBI SHNEUR ZALMAN OF LIADI, THE ALTER REBBE

When I was in my forties, I visited Masada with my son, a friend of his, and the daughter of a friend who was visiting from Montreal. As I explored a cave, I found a torn string from someone's *tzitzit* (ritual fringes). I knew that it was probably recently torn from the garment of a tourist to the site, but I couldn't help envisioning the possibility that it had been overlooked by the archeologists and historians who had excavated the site over the years and that it had in fact belonged to one of the heroes who had lived, fought, and died on the mountain. However, if it was from a tourist (the more likely possibility), that thread, connecting back to the men who had occupied the mountain two thousand years ago, testifies to the fact that they did not die in vain. The Roman Empire crumbled into debris while men with *tzitzit* still walk through the remains of the synagogue of Masada. The Roman Empire lies in ruins while the Jewish nation is still climbing Masada, wearing *tzitzit*.

And still losing *tzitzit* strings.

Have you ever noticed that you have some mitzvah that not only finds you but seems to follow you around? With me that mitzvah is *tzitzit* strings. From this Erev Yom Kippur till Motza'ei Yom Kippur (before and after Yom Kippur) alone, I found three and put them in our *genizah* pile. It was like I had to fill my quota before the end of the fast.

True, I live in a large religious area, with *baruch Hashem*, *bli ayin hara*, a lot of kids, so it's not inconceivable that there are going to be *tzitzit* strings lying on the sidewalk, but I'm pretty sure that not everyone sees them. Like Hagar, who only saw the well when Hashem's angel opened her eyes, I think these strings are attached to me and meant for my eyes only.

Many people have "their mitzvah." I met a neighbor Yom Kippur night and said to him, soon it's "your" holiday. He laughed. For Sukkot (Feast of Booths), his family goes all out — a huge *sukkah*, as much of the house brought down as possible including the kitchen sink, which we all wash at, kids' tricycles and toys, a barbecue. This neighbor and his family go on Sukkot vacation in our parking lot and, *bli ayin hara*, really do the mitzvah of rejoicing in the *chag* (holiday) properly.

Whether it's a mitzvah that chooses us or we who choose the mitzvah, each one of us has a mitzvah with our name on it, for which we are somehow destined. But we might miss it if we don't keep our eyes peeled and our hearts open. And having found it, rejoice in it like my neighbor does in his *sukkah*.

Reprinted from The Jewish Press

Betta Believe It

Until one has loved an animal, a part of one's soul remains unawakened.

ANATOLE FRANCE

When I got married, for the brief but life-altering odyssey that it would become, my husband and I got a Tiffany bowl as a wedding present. My husband said that it would be perfect for a Betta. Known as Betta splendens and nicknamed the Siamese fighting fish, Bettas are found in puddles and swamps in Southeast Asia and your local pet store. They're beautiful, decorative tropical fish seen in different vibrant colors.

So my husband got a Betta and placed the Siamese fish in an American bowl on an Israeli tray table on wooden legs from India.

The Betta lasted longer than our marriage and I never saw him again. But over the years I did buy a few Bettas as part of the menagerie of pets I got while our son was growing up.

Twenty-six years later, I decided to buy a couple of hamsters for the kids of a family in my building whom I taught English who were now moving away. I went with the mother and her youngest daughter to a pet store near my apartment. They picked out the hamsters for which I paid thirty-eight shekels, and the mother bought equipment for almost four hundred. As they were paying, I looked around and thought, "You know, God-willing, my son will be getting married soon. *God-willing. Soon.* I should bring some other life forms into the house so I won't be lonely." Now, of course a fish (or a cat or a dog or even a monkey — I've had them all as pets so I know) doesn't replace a child, but it does give you something to take care of. So I decided to buy a Betta. My neighbor was delighted and said this would be their going-away present to me.

The kids named the hamsters Alex and Yakov (two Siberian male hamsters) and I named the fish Sheffi (that's the family name of my neighbors).

I was looking for a bowl big enough and I spotted a large jar my son had bought, so I expropriated it for Sheffi. I put Sheffi in with some water and a couple of shells and watched him acclimate.

Since there wasn't a heater in the bowl (it's ninety-six degrees out!), when I turned on the air conditioning, I wrapped the bowl in a velour shawl. I fed him (a bit too often) and started talking to him.

Then I thought his bowl looked kind of empty. And I read that Bettas like to hide in grasses so on my next day running errands, I walked into a pet store and got some algae and some rocks for his bowl. Now he looks even more decorative! The enhanced décor cost twenty-five shekels. The fish had cost ten.

I'm not crazy. I'm experiencing attachment, a phenomenon that occurs with anything — plant, animal, or person — that you give a part of yourself to, whether it's money, time, affection, advice, or nurturing. When we invest ourselves in something or someone, we start to care about them. Those are the famous words of Rav Eliyahu Dessler *ztz"l*. Rabbi Dessler said that giving to someone makes you love them and that's why we love our children above anyone else, and we start talking to Bettas when we anticipate our children getting married and leaving the nest permanently. By the way, do you know that Bettas make nests by blowing minuscule bubbles? It's amazing, Divine wisdom, making a nest out of something as ephemeral as bubbles because the nest is transient and all children, if we are so blessed, leave it.

Maybe when my son gets married, I'll get him a Tiffany bowl and a Betta; carrying on a family tradition. Or maybe I'll just move in with mine.

Reprinted from The Jewish Press

To Shield and Protect

Spirituality is like a bird: if you hold it too closely, it chokes, and if you hold it too loosely, it escapes.

RAV YISRAEL SALANTER

As parents, and especially as religious parents, we try very hard to protect our children from outside sources of knowledge or influence that would be dangerous for their emotional well-being and spiritual growth. Parents each have their own limitations and boundaries. I find myself in the middle of the road on this issue. I expose my son to small amounts of things I know he'll eventually have to deal with, or will have access to, to foster his immunity and explain to him how to use them, while forbidding other things that I try to shield him from either completely or indefinitely.

But when he was nine-years-old, I got a lesson in how vulnerable we are to the world at large and how much Divine assistance is really necessary in protecting our little angels from the uglier realities of life.

I didn't allow my son to watch, listen to, or hear the news. He of course knew what was going on because in Israel the news is ubiquitously discussed, broadcast, and shared everywhere. So he heard about it on the bus, in the street, among his friends, and sometimes from me when the situation warranted it. It isn't that I wanted him to live in a cocoon or not be aware of current events, I just didn't want him to see the gory scenes or have them repeated, rehashed, and commented on four thousand times a day.

Then, one Shabbat, we went to visit friends in Ramat Beit Shemesh, an Anglo Chareidi (ultra-Orthodox) neighborhood (that's closed to traffic on Shabbat). Friday night, I went to sleep early and my son joined my friends' boys for a walk, which was supposed to include a *Shalom Zachor* (celebration of the birth of a new baby boy, the Friday night before his *brit*).

Around midnight, the boys returned and through the cobwebs of sleep, I heard my son tell his eyewitness report of a boy who had crashed a car into a wall while being pursued by police. It had exploded and an ambulance had removed the charred body from the car, all witnessed by my son.

My son had no nightmares that night, *baruch Hashem*. The next morning revealed no residual trauma and the details of the tragic incident soon became known. The car had been stolen by a Jewish, fourteen-year-old boy from the neighborhood from one of the shul's *gabba'im* (sextons). Someone had called the police, who had given chase, which marked the end of the car, the boy, and my son's innocence.

Ironically, my son told me he was more frightened by the jackal the boys allegedly saw (the neighborhood borders mountains and wilderness) and their potential encountering of scorpions and snakes that inhabit the area. Further questioning placed my child's arrival on the scene at the same time as the ambulance — i.e., after the fact.

Perhaps I was a bit naïve thinking I could protect my son from reality. There are children a lot younger than he who had spent many nights sleeping in bomb shelters and under gunfire. He was already much older when missiles started falling on Petach Tikvah.

We try to protect our children from the sordid and unpleasant realities of life, from immodest media, from the dangers that lurk behind the corners of troubled neighborhoods, from television and computers that bring it all home to them in vivid color, from literature and journalism that is less than wholesome or doesn't give over our high moral, ethical, and religious ideals, or contains graphic depictions of the horrors of crime and war, real or imagined.

And then, one Shabbos evening, in a quiet, cloistered, religious, residential neighborhood, reality strikes. Like Poe's *Mask of the Red Death*, you can't keep it out.

The truth is that though we spread our downy protective wings over our children, we can't live as ostriches. If they don't find the truth, the truth finds them. So we as enlightened, loving, religious, concerned parents of the twenty-first century may have to give greater doses of immunization so that our children are prepared when reality strikes. Parents each have to decide for themselves how much information they expose their children to, but we all have to be prepared with what to tell our children when they come to tell us what life has exposed them to.

May God keep our children safe when we are helpless to do so. And may He give us the wisdom to guide them on the safest path.

Reprinted from The Jewish Tribune UK

Picture This

Are we not like two volumes of one book?
MARCELINE DESBORDES-VALMORE

When I was at Brandeis University, my freshman student advisor was a guy who collected clocks. This was my first encounter with the American obsession of collections, my last being the castle collection my husband and I amassed during our brief marriage — which we split, when we did.

New England is a haven for antique stores and yard sales and since I enjoy antiquing, I accompanied him a couple of times on his treasure hunts.

One afternoon, we entered a clock store and while he was looking around, I looked at the pictures on the wall and found one of . . . me.

Well, it was me with much longer hair, wearing clothes from another period, but it was unmistakably me. I asked the salesman about the picture, and he said that the store's owner had picked it up at an estate sale. He wasn't around then but since the girl in the picture was so similar to me, he called the owner to come down to the store to have a look.

We waited, he arrived, and peering at the picture, he too agreed that the resemblance was uncanny. He didn't know much about the history of the picture other than where he got it, and when I offered to buy it, he refused to sell. He liked the picture. Well, that at least was flattering.

I really wanted the picture, but I was also a bit relieved he wouldn't sell it. It would have been a bit unnerving to have a picture of me when it wasn't really me. The girl in the picture was either ancient by then or long-dead and it made the hair on the back of my neck stand up.

Of course there are people in the world who look like us. We often resemble our relatives, and with about a hundred billion people having lived so far, it's conceivable that there have been other people in the world who looked like us.

Despite this, we are all unique. Even identical twins. And though I have wondered from time to time who that mysterious girl was, I am still rather busy working on deciphering who I am.

Interdisciplinary Decisions

Consilience: The linking or agreement of different disciplines when forming a theory or coming to a conclusion.

In high school, we were routinely given intelligence or interest tests so that we could start focusing on our long-term goals and limit our dreams.

I remember one time being given such a form that asked what profession I would like to pursue. There were about a dozen lines so I filled each one in with a different vocation I considered having. My classmates laughed at me. I was really just ahead of my time. Although in the 1970s people picked a profession and stuck with it for most of their lives, now it's quite common for people to switch professions or create their own by mixing disciplines.

When I was at university, I often took interdisciplinary courses like sociolinguistics, anthropological linguistics, and social psychology. These types of courses were usually more interesting and were also easier to fit into the course requirements for whatever degree you were pursuing. At the time, I was doing a B.A. in Humanistic Studies, a rather interdisciplinary degree to begin with.

I remember taking a course that had something to do with biology and ethics. The professor was a very nice older lady and she was talking about weighing decisions one against the other. The example she used was hair color. If a woman dyes her hair, the color might be toxic, but on the other hand if she didn't dye her hair, she might feel unattractive and it would affect her self-confidence, which would be bad for her mental health. She discussed pros and cons about many environmental and social issues, but hair color is what stuck with me as most relevant at the time.

But her point was that things aren't black and white, that we have to weigh the effects of both sides (or multiple sides) of every issue, and she reinforced my belief that life is indeed interdisciplinary.

As an addendum, I had the last laugh. While it's true that I didn't pursue all twelve professions, I have worked in about ten in one capacity or another. Several of them, of course, interdisciplinary.

For the Birds

The flowers appear on the earth; the time of singing is come, and the voice of the turtledove is heard in our land.

SHIR HASHIRIM 2:12

My mother's pet mitzvah was the birds. She fed them everyday rain or shine, snow or sleet. She built them a birdhouse in our maple tree in the front yard and bought them a birdbath for our backyard near our apple tree.

Wanting to perpetuate my mother's mitzvah, I bought a beautiful stone birdbath when I had an apartment with a balcony. But then my downstairs neighbor complained that the birds were messing up her patio. So I gave it away.

Fast-forward a few apartments; it was summer and the neighbor's air conditioning was dripping on my mine. The constant plink was annoying me and I was worried it would hurt the air conditioner, and my landlord was less than forthcoming when it came to fixing it.

But then I noticed something. The birds were using the pooling water to cool themselves off and relieve their parched beaks. The water from my neighbor's air conditioner had formed a birdbath.

My perspective completely changed and I started noticing the visits of not only the ubiquitous pigeons but the interloping mynah birds and exotic green parrots, who also hopped over for a visit on the neighboring unit of my bedroom window when I was working on my computer.

For the Birds

My new birdbath wasn't artistic or decorative, but it was functional. And it was provided by Divine providence. And the birds love it!

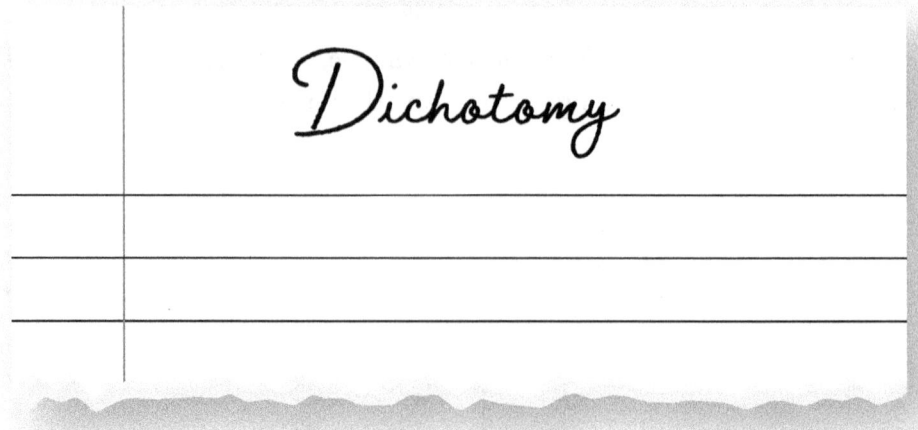

Dichotomy

Introverts unite! Individually! In your own homes!

I always thought I was an extrovert. I speak in a loud voice. I actually enjoyed performing in front of an audience, giving a presentation or a speech, and teaching. I felt no embarrassment when proposing ideas or meeting new people or initiating anything.

On the other hand, I have always hated crowds, especially large, noisy ones. I don't like being the center of attention if I'm not on stage, and I feel overwhelmed at large gatherings or parties. Ironically I feel more nervous in an audience than I do on stage.

And then I discovered you can be both — an omnivert (or ambivert) displaying extrovert characteristics in some situations and introvert characteristics in others. And thank goodness I discovered this. This dichotomy has only grown greater as I've gotten older, favoring my introverted side, and I was grateful to discover that I don't have a split personality. Apparently introverts have lower amounts of dopamine or something and have a rich inner life, so they need less outside stimulation.

Of course we're all on a continuum, but I really enjoy being classified and categorized (I know some people don't) because it provides me with greater insights about myself and makes me feel understood. I loved discovering I'm a "4" on the Enneagram when I read Miriam Adahan's book, *Awareness*. I have many leonine tendencies and although I used to be an ENFP, I think I've evolved into an INFJ.

Dichotomy

    Although, of course, we are all supposed to be evolving, knowing what you are at your core (and we all have a core personality) helps you know in which direction to grow. Although we are all complex (especially me), being understood (by ourselves and others) and gaining clarity and self-awareness is the greatest tool for self-appreciation and actualization I know of.

    And you can take my word for this because I'm a highly intuitive, ambiverted "4."

Stress and the City

A diamond is just a piece of charcoal that handled stress exceptionally well.

A few days ago I started to tell my son what happened when I was in Katzrin recently with a friend visiting from Canada.

"I know," he said. "I was with you."

Indeed he was. He came with us for our four-day sojourn to the north, only my brain had momentarily deleted that detail. I didn't know whether to laugh or cry. I've always blamed lapses in memory on my age (you know, at forty you can't remember where you left something, at fifty you can't remember what the thing you can't find is called). But it's not age; it's stress. I and everyone around me live very stressful lives. And a good percentage of that stress is self-induced. But as I toured the True North (of Israel) strong and free, looking at cascading waterfalls and the evergreen forests, and inhaling air not packed with tension, it was salubrious — mentally and physically.

For many years now, I have dreamed of living up north. My friends say I'd be bored (God-willing). It is true that since I keep the pace of a squirrel two weeks before hibernation, slowing my pace would be a little challenging. But I have always been up to a challenge and anyway, it's not the speed and rhythm of life that makes it stressful, it's the multitasking, the immediacy, the bombardment of the senses that render us all constantly overwhelmed.

A relatively new innovation on Israeli buses is a recorded announcement of the bus stops — the stop you just left, the stop coming up, and the stop you're at. It's annoying! I admit it's helpful to visually impaired people and people taking the bus for the first time (and multitasking people who can't look out the window), but what happened to talking to people on the bus? Social alienation is another cause of stress. Of course, social interaction is also a form of stress. Especially in Israel.

I came to Israel in 1982. In 1982 there were still public phones, which you had to use because there was a dearth of private phones. Office equipment consisted of the typewriter; I wrote letters to my friends using paper and pen at home and then went to mail them at the post office. The fax machine was the cutting edge of new technology at the time.

I was at a wedding recently and everyone at my table had their cell phones on the table and they were checking their messages every few minutes. At least part of the time, they weren't present. Being two places at once equals stress!! (Unless you're letting your mind wander during a lecture or doing something relaxing, unless you have to take a test on it.)

Do they not have these things up north? They do. You get reception even while looking at the coypus munching grass with their orange teeth at the Hula Lake. You can even take a picture of them and send it to your friends in the city on your cell phone. But no one is rushing anywhere. The combination of fewer people per square kilometer, the soothing nepenthe of nature, and the choice of living a slower life lead to the fact that you actually experience life instead of rushing in a blur through it.

On a visit to the zoo once, I was informed that the reason tortoises live so long is that they move slowly.

I grew up in St. Laurent, a suburb of Montreal, where the most excitement was a snowstorm in winter and a hailstorm in summer. I longed for, craved, desired excitement and adventure, but I got jaded fast. Well, not that fast; I was young but I would love to return to the pace of my youth, where just sitting with someone on the grass was called an activity and you actually had their full attention. This bombardment of noise, information, and activity is eroding our priorities. City life offers many conveniences and opportunities, but it also offers endless things we "must" do at the expense of those things we should do. People in cities, especially young people in cities, spend a lot of time running needless laps in the rat race. And we, the human race, are getting nowhere fast (technological advances aside).

I mean do we really care what people whom we haven't seen in thirty years are having for lunch? Is it really necessary to eschew spending actual time with friends to go on Facebook? Must we really text while we're talking to our spouses, children, and grandparents?

I'm lucky I'm religious; I get at least one day a week off this craziness. But 24/6 is still enough to erode my senses. And it does.

All kinds of practical considerations may mean that I only get up north once or twice a year until I retire, but if I want to get to the age of retirement with most of my faculties intact, even though I can't go back to a simpler time, I can try and simplify my life. And if we all try to do that, we might actually have a chance at remembering what we did and with whom we did it.

First published in the Metro supplement of The Jerusalem Post

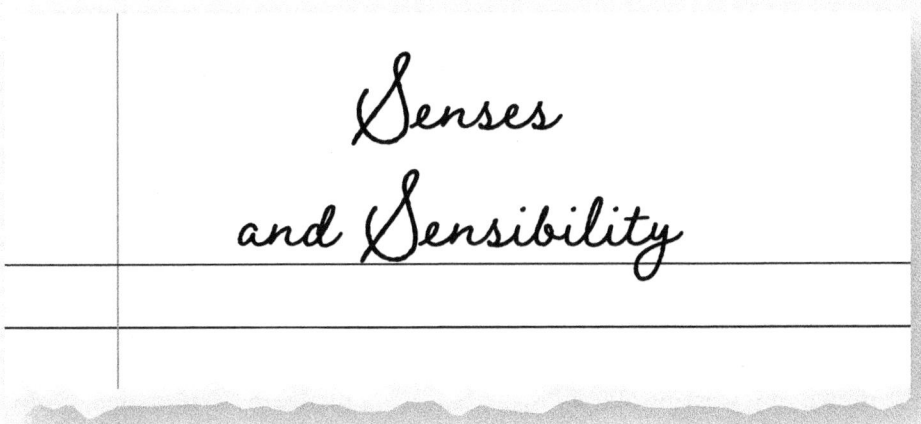

Senses and Sensibility

As for hearing, the sloth is not so much deaf as uninterested in sound.

YANN MARTEL

The coating on my glasses had peeled off, blurring my vision. As I had a guarantee on the veneer, I took it to the store to have it redone. In the meantime, I put on a pair of glasses from a previous prescription. They were just a bit weaker. And something amazing happened. I suddenly felt calmer. Everything seemed less immediate, less urgent. And you know what else — I didn't need the multifocal lens I had for reading. My reading wasn't blurred anymore.

My son, who also wanted new glasses, had a new prescription filled. But when he put on the glasses, he complained they were too strong and gave him a headache. He said he wanted to try and get them to change them to his previous prescription. The next day though, he told me he would try to get used to them. He did and says he sees much sharper. Now, he needs to get new contact lenses.

The next day, I went to a *simchah*. The music was blaring at such a high volume I'm certain that it caused a tsunami in some part of the world. We asked them to tone it down; I put paper in my ears, but it still was unendurably loud.

What is it about today's society that requires that we see things the sharpest, hear things the loudest, and have the most highly defined sensual experiences? We overcorrect our vision, amplify our music to unheard-of decibels, and there must be hundreds of types of perfumes on the markets. It's like we can't get enough sensory stimulation while we're already suffering the consequences of overload. Then we get used to the overload and require even more heightened experiences for our senses, which get increasingly dulled.

What happened to appreciation of the muted pastels of Impressionism; the pleasure of birds and crickets chirping? We are awash in a sea of sensory stimuli that is wearing out our nerve endings and making us both demanding and frazzled.

It is the result of living in a world hungry for perfection and never satiated, looking for higher, deeper, sharper, better, yet ironically dulling our senses.

And it isn't necessary. The eye test you have to pass to get a driver's license or join the army is much less than 20/20 vision. The physical acuity that you need to survive is much lower than what the average person aims for.

This goes for thrills of a lifetime, too. They're building faster, higher, and more dangerous roller coasters because we've already become inured to the thrills and chills of the previous ones. I personally hate roller coasters and don't put one nerve ending on them.

There's a point at which we have to stop striving to be superhuman or experience super-fidelity and super-thrills before we lose our ability to perceive subtlety. Maybe this need to tone things down is a function of age. But with age also comes wisdom and maybe it's wise to take the edge off. We don't have to see, hear, and thrill to everything. We'd probably be happier with a little more subtlety and sensory ignorance. A bit of haze and quiet.

When I got my glasses back, I was able better to appreciate the experience of seeing with greater clarity because I had learned to be comfortable with less than perfection.

To paraphrase John F. Kennedy, ask not what intensity life can give to you, ask how you can intensify life for others. If we stop demanding the height of sensory experience from the world and start giving the best of ourselves back, both we and the world will reach amazing heights.

Disclaimer: This is not an endorsement for not wearing appropriate corrective lenses or hearing aids when required or not taking your kids to amusement parks.

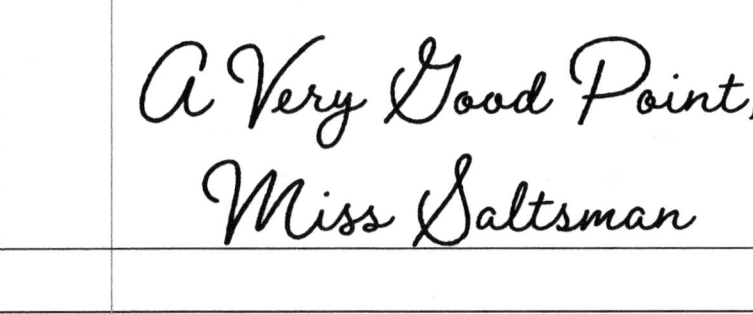

A Very Good Point, Miss Saltsman

And all the knowledge we possess
We mutually impart

W.S. GILBERT

In the course of my education, I have taken many, many classes and learned many things. Some I even remember, most of which have nothing to do with academics. One of the professors who made a great impression on me was from the Department of Education at McGill University. I had him for one semester for one class, which was compulsory for everyone doing a Diploma in Education — Philosophy of Education.

The subject was often boring but he was riveting. He had a booming voice and lots of energy and he treated us with respect. He called all the students by their last name with a title. No one had ever experienced this in class before. This was before Harry Potter was published.

Not only did he address us with our surnames, but it was always preceded with a compliment. "That's a very good question, Mr. Thomas." "That's a very good point, Miss Saltsman," and "Thank you for your input."

Being young, we smirked, but we all enjoyed it. And I learned more about making a student feel valued from him than from any other teacher. And it wasn't like he even had a personal relationship with any of us.

There was an audition I really wanted to go to. I think it was to do a summer theater program in Banff (I didn't get in). But the date of the audition conflicted with one of his exams. When I asked if there was some way I could do the exam another day, he willingly agreed. This was university, not high school.

Apropos his tests — I remember their being easy short answer tests of about a hundred questions. But what was special was how he marked them. He didn't just put an X besides any wrong answers. He put a tick beside every right answer so that you had 96 ticks with four Xs. And of course he added some encouraging comments, both beside the answers and at the bottom of the test.

I learned how to mark from this professor. And in all my years as a teacher (okay not that many), I marked as per his example.

I don't really remember too much about the different educational philosophies the class was meant to introduce me to. Neither do I care to, but I do remember I learned a lot about how to be a good teacher.

Global Positioning Spiritually

Choices are the hinges of destiny

EDWIN MARKHAM

A colleague at work ordered a GPS from China. It came, it went to Romania, it came back, it didn't work; he sent it back to China. It came back better than new. This colleague is a gentleman and he often gave me a lift home even though he had to go out of his way to do it. He said it was only a few minutes and he didn't mind. Ever since he had gotten his new technology, the GPS, he liked to have it on in the car, just to make sure it was working. Only it was set with the destination of his home so that every time it gave an instruction and the instruction was ignored (because he was driving me home), the GPS said, "Recalculating route." In the course of the drive home, it may have said this about twenty times. I was waiting for it to yell, "You idiot, you're going the wrong way!" But it didn't. In the same digital, soothing voice it said (in Hebrew), "Recalculating route."

It occurred to me, on one of these drives home, that our spiritual GPS works the same way. When we follow a path we aren't meant to, either because it's wrong or wrong for us or won't lead us where we're supposed to go, we get a signal that we've veered off course. Usually it takes the form of our plans not working out or some other glitch, be it professional, financial, or interpersonal. It isn't delivered in a soothing voice, but we're supposed to respond to it the same way and recalculate our course with the same equanimity as the automobile's GPS. Imagine missing a bus or getting upsetting news, and instead of complaining saying, "Recalculating route."

The really unique thing about the GPS, though, is that no matter how far away you get from your destination, it can still lead you back to where you need to be. There's always a starting point back in the right direction.

That's reassuring because sometimes I can stray way off-course, completely losing my sense of direction. But there's always that Guiding and Positioning System pointing me in the right direction, as I recalculate my route.

First published in The Jewish Press

Divine Choreography

Every dance has a purpose and every dancer has a destiny.
OLIVER PHIPPS

When I was in my forties, I took a flamenco class. I always wanted to dance flamenco. One of the girls in the class made a disparaging comment about my dancing. My feathers were very ruffled, and only after the teacher reassured me that my dancing was fine and the girl apologized profusely having meant no harm . . . did it continue to bother me. But I danced on the other side of the room from her and, a few months later, left the class because it was no longer convenient to take it.

Fast-forward a couple of years. A very good friend of mine invited me to come bring joy to a bride and groom. The bride was a *giyoret* (convert) and the groom was a *ba'al teshuvah* (newly religious). They didn't have much family, so it was a mitzvah to attend. Lack of energy almost prevented me from going even though the wedding was being held in a *shul* nearby, but in the end I went. The bride was glowing and greeted me very warmly. "Don't you remember me?" she asked. It was the girl from the flamenco class. I danced enthusiastically that night and was finally able to forgive her, paradoxically, by dancing at her wedding.

First published as part of a longer article in The Jewish Press

Nahafochu*

It is not as man sees – man sees what his eyes behold, but God sees into the heart.

SHMUEL I 16:7

A good friend (let's call her Amy) sent me an email about a spiritual dilemma she had.

A very disheveled man with almost no teeth, very dirty clothes, and a *kippah* on his head was in the cashier's line in front of her and another woman. All he had in his shopping cart were ten bottles of wine and about twenty huge cans of Similac (baby formula).

My friend turned to the woman in front of her and told her that she felt very sad looking at this man, automatically assuming that he was buying all that stuff as a mitzvah to distribute in some very poor neighborhood.

A third woman came over and said, "Are you kidding?! That wine and Similac is on sale here for a fifty percent discount, and he's buying it for his store where he is going to resell it and make a profit!"

This woman didn't explain how she thought a man who looked like that owned a store. Nor did she account for the fact that a person who does run a store buys merchandise from wholesalers at a cheaper price than a retailer would sell even on sale; however, ignorance is one of the usual preconditions of *lashon hara* (evil speech), but back to our story.

Until that point nothing unseemly of this nature had occurred to my friend (although even if it were true, it's not a crime), but when she looked

*A situation that's turned upside down

Nahafochu

at him again, the doubts set in. He had one of those gift cards that you purchase, so she wondered where he got the cash. And then she wondered how he knew to come to buy just those two items in large quantities. And how did he get to Ramat Aviv Gimmel (the scene of the story), and how was he going to get all that heavy stuff home?

Ramat Aviv Gimmel is a largely affluent and secular suburb of Tel Aviv, where the man and his purchase obviously stood out.

Amy went from being so sad to thinking that this guy was now going to take advantage of people poorer than he was. So she asked him why he was buying all that stuff, and he said it was for a kindergarten. "And the wine is also for the kindergarten?" she probed.

"No. That isn't," he answered politely, without elaborating.

She realized it wasn't even any of her business, but she couldn't rid herself of the feeling that she had somehow been duped by judging him favorably even though there was no evidence contradicting her original assumption.

Amy told the story to a few people and, interestingly enough, each person had their own take on it. One person (obviously not someone who lives in Israel) thought that he sounded like a drunk who had a baby to support; and Amy's daughter thought the man was poor and was buying the Similac for nourishment because it was cheap.

She asked me what I thought and I told her that how she and the people she spoke to had viewed that man is more a reflection of them than the man. This was a perfect example of the Ba'al Shem Tov's teaching that the world is our mirror, reflecting back to us who we are.

There used to be this old beggar man who stood outside the stores in my neighborhood on Fridays. I was sure he was Eliyahu Hanavi (Elijah the prophet), and I always tried to give him money even if it meant going home and coming back. One day I was in the post office and he was outside and a woman came in yelling about how they shouldn't let vagrants near the post office and how he could be dangerous, etc.

Now I'm willing to concede that he may not have been Eliyahu Hanavi, but I was positive he was probably less dangerous than she was.

This man Amy was describing didn't need to be judged favorably. He wasn't doing anything wrong, just incongruous. It sounded to me as though someone had perhaps given him this card as *tzedakah* and he was using it to fulfill a basic need in a poor religious area — baby food and wine for Kiddush (blessing made on wine on Shabbat). Or maybe *he* was Eliyahu Hanavi. The point is that given the same situation, many people came up with interpretations that were completely different, if not totally opposite.

Amy pointed out that no one knew the truth but him. But that's not the issue. The issue is that one person saw him as a struggling Jew doing a mitzvah and another person saw him as an opportunist taking advantage of poor people.

It's interesting that on Purim we're supposed to give charity to anyone who proffers his hand and not question or investigate their motives, something we are allowed to do the rest of the year. That's because the Purim story, where everything changed in a minute, taught us that things are not always what they appear to be. In fact, they seldom are and nobody knows the truth about anything except God, which is why most of the time, unless there are very incriminating circumstances, we're supposed to judge people positively and give them the benefit of the doubt. God knows it's hard for us, when we're always going around judging people in our heads, to withhold judgment, so He cautions us at least to judge favorably even if it's difficult.

I have no doubt that the man in question was somehow involved with *chesed*. He either received it or gave it, or both.

My friend made the very valid point of how scary it is that a person's perspective can be turned on its head by an unthinking (and unfeeling) remark. We have to be very careful not to be influenced by other people's negative interpretations. Because things are seldom what they seem even, and perhaps especially, in a dissonant situation.

What is encouraging is that my friend saw a huge spiritual and practical lesson to be learned here, and she felt like it represented something so deep that she kept mulling it over and discussing it with everyone she talked to in the next few hours. Something along the lines of how our reality can be changed in a millisecond, and how a person's world can be set spinning so easily. *Nahafochu!*

May we always remember to see the good in people and that things are much deeper and more complex than they appear on the surface, and if we're going to judge, to judge positively because, as Amy always likes to say, what goes around comes around.

First published in The Jewish Press

Your greatest contribution may not be something you do but someone you raise.

ANDY STANLEY

My son and I were having Shabbat dinner with friends when a minor dispute broke out between two of the adorable grandchildren of our hosts, who are a few months apart and around two years old. Many are familiar with the rather clever poem "The Toddler's Creed" by Dr. Burton L. White: "If I want it, it's mine! If I give it to you and change my mind later, it's mine! If I can take it away from you, it's mine! If it's mine it will never belong to anybody else, no matter what . . . ."

And in keeping with this epic yet prosaic poem, one of the boys (who usually get along quite well for toddler cousins) grabbed a water bottle from the other. And then the wronged child burst into tears as anticipated. But I noticed that these were deep, heartfelt, "my world has been destroyed" tears. And that's when I had an incredibly deep, epiphanous insight. It couldn't have been the water that was the problem; we had a table full of food and drink. I don't even think it was the injustice. What that cry seemed to me to signify was the deep pain of being discounted, of not seeming to matter, of having oneself and one's needs be rendered invisible, not worthy of attention. And the little tyke calmed down when he was cuddled and soothed; that is, as soon as someone else gave him back the feeling of importance, that someone showed he cares about his feelings.

That Motza'ei Shabbat, I was emptying some papers from a box into my desk (having recently moved again) and I came across a drawing a student once did of me while I was teaching. It was actually a brilliant rendition. She drew me singing while holding a deck of cards, asking if anyone wanted to see a card trick; the Mary Poppins–style carpetbag I used to carry was on the floor beside me and a knocked-over bottle of Coke was on the table. Although it was sketched in black and white, in that one picture she painted me in many colors. I was funny and entertaining, sugar-addicted, clumsy, whimsical (and unusually thin). She saw me and I felt validated! And long after I finally throw out some of the papers my son is begging me to get rid of, I will hold on that drawing by a student who probably already has kids of her own. Because she *saw* me.

And it struck me that the cause of all pain and despair, depression and anger, violence and crime, arguments and feuds, lack of self-esteem and hopelessness, divorce and estrangement is not being acknowledged and validated, respected and cared about. I'm not talking only about neglect and abuse. I'm talking about the landlord ignoring his tenant's plea to fix a leaky faucet. I'm talking about the boss who repeatedly ignores the employee's extra efforts at work. I'm talking about the husband who takes his wife for granted and doesn't notice her, and the parent who throws her children's artwork into the trash or ignores their attempts to engage her in conversation. I'm talking about the person who brashly pushes ahead in line and the rude caller who puts someone on hold to answer call waiting. I'm talking about the doctor or friend who keeps people waiting for over an hour and the person who impatiently cuts the person they're talking to off mid-sentence. I'm talking about the person who yells at another driver for their perceived traffic violation or the man who won't put his cigarette out when asked. I'm talking about the insensitive clerk and the oversensitive plaintive. I'm talking about the person who won't hold the door for another or who doesn't say thank you to the person who does.

Isn't that what the students of Rabbi Akiva were punished for? Not honoring one another? To honor someone doesn't only mean to give them an award or always use their proper title. It means having *derech eretz* (manners), behaving with the most basic of manners and fundamental cordiality. It means making the other person feel seen, heard, and validated.

Because when we don't receive this most basic recognition, we scream and cry — if not outside then inside, and if not then and there, then later and maybe even at someone else. And all these cries and tears go up to the Heavenly throne and then God forbid, terrible things can happen if we don't show enough deference and caring to one another, if we act like other people and their thoughts and feelings don't matter.

Every unkind or insensitive word and action cuts deep and leaves a terrible scar. If you think I'm overreacting, notice your reaction the next time someone slights you or leaves you feeling unseen, unheard, or like you don't matter. And then, please forgive them and strive to do better. Our number one need from the moment we are born to the moment we leave this world is to feel worthy, liked, appreciated, and valued. And every time someone robs us of that feeling it's like, well, taking a bottle from a toddler, and the reaction is raw and visceral even if it's covered by a façade of maturity.

So let us all strive for greater heights by recognizing the worth of every individual we come into contact with and doing something to raise their spirits by giving them a feeling of self-worth. And then watch the transformation in them and in you.

And if you want, I'd be happy to show you a card trick.

First published in The Jewish Press

God Is with Me

> Behold! The bush was burning in the fire but the bush was not consumed.
>
> SHEMOT 3:2

The truth is that I'm a very neurotic person. I check to make sure that the gas and stove are off, sometimes several times, before leaving the house. And that's when I haven't even turned it on for a couple of days. I do this again before going to sleep at night, and I stare at the Shabbos candles willing them to reassure me that they will not go anywhere if I'm invited somewhere for dinner Friday night.

I was very anxious about which yeshiva to send my son to for seventh grade. I agonized about it. One Wednesday night, I went to a lecture with a friend given by the *rosh yeshiva* (head of the yeshiva) of one of the schools I was contemplating. After the lecture, I discussed the issue with my friend. As we parted, she said, "Don't worry, God is with you."

"God is with me," I repeated nervously.

I went upstairs to my apartment. My son had decided to go to sleep while I was at the lecture. He was old enough to stay alone and as I was literally only a few minutes away, I didn't worry too much.

I barely smelled it as I walked in the house, but there seemed to be the smell of something burning. I hadn't cooked anything. Then horror gripped me as I remembered. I had put some vegetarian schnitzel in the oven a couple of hours earlier to warm up. My son had wanted some and we had both forgotten about it and, uncharacteristically, I hadn't checked the stove before I left.

My son had been sleeping soundly and the schnitzel was burnt to a crisp. No smoke, no fire, *baruch Hashem*, just burnt schnitzel. A cold dread gripped my heart as the thought flitted through my numbed brain of what God-forbid might have happened.

There was a clear message here. Actually there were two. It isn't my compulsive checking that keeps me safe because God can arrange it that I forget to check. The second, more obvious one, is that it's God Who is keeping me and my son safe.

I was sure that He would also help me decide on the best educational course for my son. And He did! *Baruch Hashem*!

God is with me, with us, always, and I am so very, very grateful!

First published in The Jewish Tribune UK
Also published in Eternally Grateful

Life Is in the Details

Home is the school where we learn that love shows itself in the details.

ANDI ASHWORTH

I hate details. I'm more of an intuitive, big picture person. I find details annoying, bothersome, boring, intimidating, overwhelming...

But then I realized something — life is details. Raising a child, running a home, writing a book, running a business, having relationships are all about details, millions and millions of them that add up to your life.

Raising children is about billions of kisses, millions of hugs, thousands of feedings, and hundreds of signatures. Running a business is about invoices and bills, tracking customers and buying stamps. Writing is about remembering to buy paper for the printer and maintaining your computer as well as a good relationship with your computer maintenance man. Running a home is about running out to buy milk and paying the bills, and having a long, lasting relationship with someone is more than anything about the details. Friendships are the total of endless emails, long-lost letters, and continuous conversations involving details. Tradition, religion, and faith are about a myriad of details. The body of each one of us is a microcosm of details and the universe is a macrocosm of details. It's like a Seurat painting. Billions of colorful dots that come together to make the brilliant work of the art of our lives. Each of us is a pointillist masterpiece. I keep crying, "Spare me the details," but if I were spared, I would be spared a good deal of life.

Grand gestures are very dramatic but they are few and far between, and usually they too are the culmination of hundreds of details that came before. It is no wonder that as science and technology increase their wisdom, they discover more and more details. The vaster, the more minute, the more important something is, the more details it involves. And nothing is more vast or intricate than life. The more we are involved with the particulars, the deeper we are involved with the nuclei of our existence. When we look back at our lives, we recall certain details vividly and forget others just as vividly. But they all matter.

Details are often tedious, frequently tiresome, and always necessary. They are the minutiae whose sum equals the whole. We can, of course, delegate many details to other people. And often this is necessary in living our lives as efficiently as possible. On the other hand, aren't the most special moments of life, the ones we celebrate and remember, details? Our baby's first smile, our first kiss, the first scent of spring, a summer rain, a new winter snowfall, a royalty check in the mail, a family joke. We can relieve ourselves of some of life's tedium by entrusting the less desirable finer points to someone else's charge. But in the process, we could also be sacrificing the rewards entailed therein.

Attention to detail means we have a life and it's full . . . of details.

The Elixir of Encouragement

Looking fifty is great, if you're sixty.
                                                                JOAN RIVERS

I hate exercise! I don't mean something fun like walking or dancing, I mean the kind you share with other not-quite-in-shape women, stretching and groaning, trying to thin out your body by thickening your muscles exercise. But it was either that or give up chocolate and carbohydrates, heaven forefend, and the class was about thirty meters from my apartment, easy access, almost the same distance as the supermarket where I stock up on chocolate and carbohydrates. So I went.

The regular teacher went on vacation and we had a replacement. This woman quickly learned my name and used it to dole out portions of encouragement exclaiming at my remarkable flexibility. "Look at Rosally," she'd croon. All of a sudden I was extending superhuman effort trying to reach even further in the direction she indicated, looking for another opportunity to be heaped with praise. I even went twice a week, looking forward to being told I'm flexible. Now to be clear, one thing I'm definitely not, literally or figuratively, is flexible. But all of a sudden this woman said I was and so I was. And it was wonderful!

Positive reinforcement has always yielded better results than criticism and censure. Moreover, it makes that which is seemingly impossible possible. It underscores the incredible power of belief. Miracles are nurtured with belief, with faith and trust, and giving voice to these qualities provides positive reinforcement, armed with which anyone can do anything.

Okay, it's true I had to lie down a few times because I had overexerted. But when I was moving, I was unstoppable because someone else believed me to be.

Each one of us knows how it feels to cringe at condemnation and preen at praise. We all know the empyrean heights we can reach on the wings of acclaim. But the rub is that we are dependent on one another to provide this soul food. We need to feed each other encouragement in order to survive emotionally. Students need it from teachers, children from parents, spouses from each other, employees from bosses, and each of us from one another. And as with any mitzvah, we get to share in the dividends. The achievements that people attain, applauded by us, belong in part to us as well. When we raise people up, they elevate us too and there is no limit to what heights we can reach together.

I don't know how much bodybuilding I achieved with this teacher, but I know she built up something much more important.

First appeared in The Jewish Press

Habitat

And that unusual squawking sound is actually the mating call of the rare...oh, it's just an oboe player.

STEVE IRWIN

Driving down a highway early in my marriage, my husband stopped because he had seen a tortoise crossing the highway and wanted to take it home. As much as I liked the creature, I argued that we were in Canada and, living in New York, it wouldn't be feasible to take it over the border. In any case, it was a free tortoise and should continue enjoying its freedom (although it probably would have enjoyed a longer life as a pet rather than crossing a highway).

When we came across a pet store back in New York that sold every manner of reptile, amphibian, and creepy-crawly, I thought this would be a good opportunity to make it up to him, and one day I surprised my husband with a tortoise.

The tortoise didn't do very much and when, for a long period of time, he didn't move, I just assumed he was hibernating. But on second thought, I took him back to the store, where they informed me that he wasn't sleeping, he was sick. Not enough sun, apparently.

Oh. I had thought that cold-blooded creatures didn't like the sun, so I had kept him in the shade. I was wrong; cold-blooded creatures need the sun to heat up their bodies enough to move. By depriving the solar-powered tortoise of sunshine, I had nearly killed him. Once he was hale and hearty again, the store called us to come and get him. But I told them to keep him, on us, as I was returning to Israel and still had to find another arrangement for the hamsters, their progeny, and a Siamese fighting fish.

I wanted to contribute to a lemur exhibit at the Jerusalem zoo and asked how much it cost. I was told it costs millions of shekels. Apparently recreating a "natural" habitat is a costly endeavor. But it's necessary for the exhibit's animals not only to survive but to thrive.

Although mammals are the most adaptable creatures, even though we can't do that starfish thing of re-growing an appendage, and although humans are the most adaptable of God's creations, each one of us also needs the right habitat for survival as well as quality of life: specific types of food, adequate rest, a home environment that reflects our physical, emotional, and spiritual needs, time and space to regroup, and the right balance of friends and family for our personality type.

Desmond Morris wrote a groundbreaking (or at least entertaining) sociology book called *The Human Zoo*. In it, he talks about how urban life goes against the natural lifestyle of humans and how all of society's ills can be attributed to people being forced to live in overcrowded cities.

As I mentioned above, we are all different species of animal. And we all have specific needs for our unique temperaments, personalities, and preferences. Recognizing this, and respecting it, will contribute much to our well-being and that of those with whom we share our lives.

A portion of this article first appeared in The Jewish Tribune UK

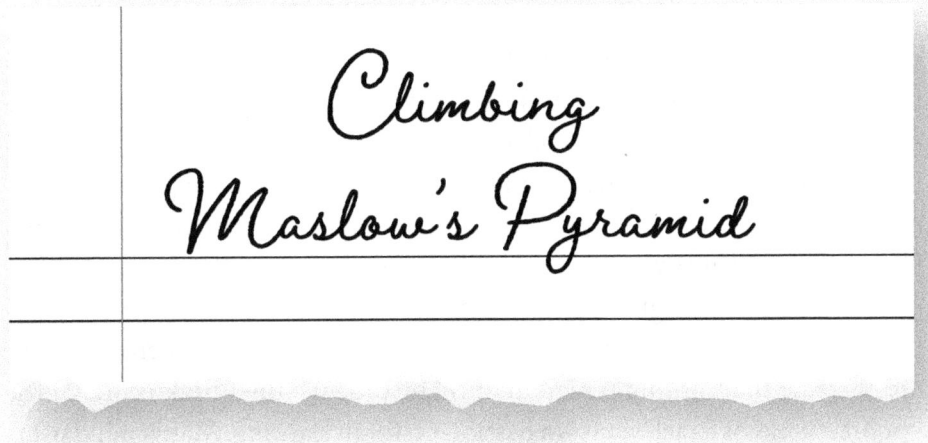

Climbing Maslow's Pyramid

Creativity is intelligence having fun.

ALBERT EINSTEIN

Anyone who has taken Psychology 101 has heard of Maslow's Hierarchy of Needs, also referred to as Maslow's Pyramid because it is usually depicted as such.

Dr. Abraham Maslow was a psychologist who identified the universal needs of every human being and classified them going from most basic to highest. His claim was that a person would not be able to realize his true potential, and attend to his higher needs, unless his lower needs were met. For example, someone who is on the brink of starvation will not worry about getting his doctorate (unless trying to get his doctorate is the cause of his starvation).

Maslow's hierarchy lists human needs in this order: Physiological needs (food, water, air); Safety needs (shelter from cold, rain, snow, katyusha rockets); Love and belonging needs (friends, family, community); Esteem needs (a job, appreciation, a title); Self-Actualization needs (reaching one's creative potential, having one's article published).

On the surface, Maslow's argument makes sense. One occupied with basic survival will not have the time or energy to worry about making the social register, being published, or receiving the Nobel Prize. The ephemeral would be eclipsed by the basic physiological requirements of existence.

Although Dr. Maslow's model is one of the few things I remember from Psychology 101, it is easy to disprove. Firstly, much of the world's art and literature has come from people starving in garrets and living hand to mouth under leaky roofs. Need proof? Just go have a look at a Van Gogh or listen to Mozart. We wouldn't have much of our literature, art, and music if it weren't for starving writers, artists, and musicians living in angst and poverty.

L'havdil, there are many brilliant Torah commentaries that were written by rabbis living in poverty and cold and suffering persecution. Moreover, they claimed that their high level of erudition was a direct result of their poverty and, even today, many yeshivas purposely maintain a Spartan environment to increase the learning potential of their students. Bnei Brak is one of the poorest areas of Israel, yet it is a bastion of Torah learning. Many of Judaism's greatest men and women were people who lived in meager circumstances, yet rose above them to achieve a level of spiritual actualization that Maslow couldn't even imagine. Moreover, in many cases it was not in spite of, but because of, their dire circumstances that they rose to the high spiritual levels that they did.

But the main thing wrong with Maslow's premise is that it goes counter to the basic tenets of Judaism. According to Judaism, the greatest level of self-actualization is achieving closeness to God. And the way to achieve closeness to God is to perform mitzvahs, the 613 commandments. Mitzvahs have no prerequisite preconditions. You do not need to be rich or even have a roof over your head to do a mitzvah. A person who doesn't have a lot to eat but makes a blessing on the food and shares it with others has sanctified both the food and himself before God. A person who doesn't earn much money but tithes it to share with those less well-off than himself has performed an act of selflessness that defies his lower nature.

Maslow's premise, that we can only reach the higher parts of ourselves when our lowest needs have been met, doesn't take into account our Divine soul. It reduces our soul to the level of an animal. People have the tremendous capacity to overcome their circumstances and act in noble and Godly ways even when they don't have many resources at their disposal.

Many stories have been written about the self-sacrifice of Jews during the Holocaust to perform mitzvahs and acts of kindness. But we don't have to go so far back. Roi Klein, the Israeli soldier who jumped on a grenade in July 2006 to save his fellow soldiers, relinquished his safety needs for a higher goal, the highest goal, saving the life of another. All the volunteers who helped families huddling in shelters when they were under missile attack did not wait until it was safe to do so. Clearly personal safety was not a precondition for these people to achieve self-actualization.

Yom Kippur, the holiest day of the year, is the time when most Jews reach their highest point of transcendence. This is done not only in spite of the fact that they have no food or water for twenty-five hours but because of it. They are able to humble themselves before their Creator when they overcome their most basic physical desires in order to serve Him.

And while there is no question that friends and family enrich our lives, achieving success is not predicated upon their existence. Israel was built by the orphans of the Holocaust who, bereft of family, friends, and any relic of their past identities, built the land of Israel physically and spiritually.

It would appear then that Maslow's pyramid lacks a solid foundation. Jewish history has shown that there is nothing that can stop a Jew from reaching the top and rising above his physical limitations when he connects to his spiritual essence.

First published in JewishWorldReview.com

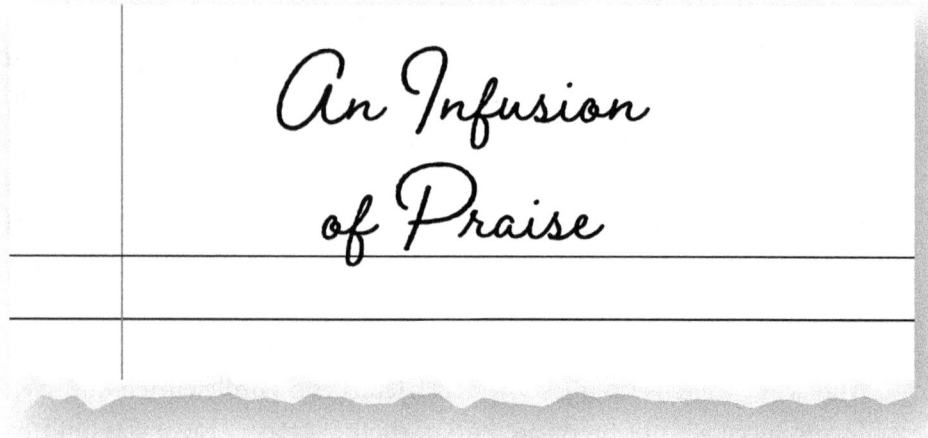

An Infusion of Praise

I find the greatest reward for doing is the opportunity to do more.

DR. JONAS SALK

Apart from the five years when I was banned because of a bout with Hepatitis A, I have been giving blood regularly since my friend Sandra ran a blood drive at McGill University, when I was nineteen. A friend and neighbor who donates plasma regularly suggested I do likewise. He said that it's more important than giving blood.

Well, I went to the blood bank and had a blood test done. The doctor told me I was an excellent candidate for donating plasma because I have a high thrombocyte count.

There was something about the way he said it, too. Enraptured. And then he told the secretary that my thrombocyte level was over 400. "Really?! 400?" She looked impressed.

Now I must tell you that I had no idea what thrombocytes are. Having worked and volunteered in hospitals had done nothing to raise my medical awareness. But I was beaming. I didn't care what thrombocytes were. I was brimming with them, and they were in demand.

The doctor then explained that they were needed for cancer patients undergoing chemotherapy. I knew from my neighbor that they can be donated more often than blood. The doctor told me I was eligible to give

An Infusion of Praise

plasma three months after my last blood donation — and to eat red meat, as my hemoglobin level was low.

While I no doubt felt elated about the prospect of doing a special mitzvah, I was also basking in the reflected glory of my elevated thrombocyte level, a fact that has little to do with me, I have no part in, and I had no previous awareness of.

There ought to be a praise bank — a place where people who need a boost to the immune system of their self-esteem can come and be commended by people ready to donate compliments. Though it is a lot less uncomfortable than being pricked by a needle, for some reason, blood donations are often more forthcoming than donations of praise. Yet they are no less vital to our continued existence and our quality of life.

I'm not suggesting that people stop giving the gift of life. But maybe we can devote a little time each day to making donations of encouragement and praise to enhance the *quality* of life. There is no prerequisite minimum hemoglobin level, thrombocyte, or set cell count of any type or color. And, similarly, there is no prerequisite minimum of encouragement to be offered.

In addition, we can give this precious gift every day, not only once in a while.

I ended up giving plasma only a couple of times and went back to giving blood as the smallness of my veins made the longer donation time a bit difficult. But if you can do it, that's great! And if you can't, please give blood.

"Your blood is replaceable. A life is not."

First published in The Jewish Tribune UK

Choices

*Two roads diverged in a wood, and I —
I took the one less traveled by,
And that has made all the difference.*

ROBERT FROST

I love to travel, but I don't get to do it much anymore. I just don't have the money. Actually, that isn't strictly true. I do have the money but I use it to publish my books. Well, that's not strictly true either. I don't have the money but since publishing my books is a priority, I somehow find the money to supplement whatever I fundraise.

I believe that there's no such thing as "can't." There are priorities and choices and prices to pay but basically, and history — personal and national — has proven this millions of times over, there's no can't.

I once had an argument with a woman who claimed she didn't have the money to send her children to a Jewish school. She and her husband were professionals; they owned their own home and weren't eligible for a break in tuition (which admittedly is very high in the United States). So what was the problem? She told me that if she sent her kids to a Jewish school, they wouldn't be able to pay for other things like taking their kids to Disneyland.

So they took their kids to Disneyland and didn't send them to a Jewish school, and now both kids have intermarried because the message they were given was that Disneyland is more important than Judaism.

I once saw a program, many years ago during the height of the Russian *aliyah*, about a couple who decided that they couldn't bear seeing all their money go for rent and bills. They worked hard, but they didn't have enough money to give their son the good life they wanted to. So they stopped renting an apartment and pitched a tent in Gan Ha'atzmaut in Tel Aviv, which is right near the sea.

Since they didn't need the money for rent and bills anymore, they used it to give their son any extracurricular activity he wanted. They signed him up for surfing lessons, for example, and they were able to enjoy barbecues in the park whenever they wanted. There were two drawbacks to this lifestyle. Someone always had to stay in the tent — the three of them couldn't go out together because they risked having all their possessions stolen; and they didn't have a refrigerator (which would need electricity), so they had to buy all their food fresh daily.

But it was worth it for them. Their priority was to give their son the good life and for them it didn't mean an apartment, it meant giving him all the extras. Education is a primary value in Russia, and learning to surf was more important than having indoor plumbing. So they happily made the exchange. I don't know how many years they lived this way, but I'm betting their child had an amazing childhood and learned the value of living life to the fullest.

I got divorced before I found out I was pregnant, so I was a single mother from day one. For me, it was very important to be with my child all the time and not put him in any kind of daycare until he started pre-kindergarten. So, for the most part, I didn't work in those formative years. And I nursed him for the first two and a half. Was this easy? No. *Baruch Hashem* I had some major financial miracles during that time, but I also went into debt. Because being a full-time mother was my priority and I was willing to pay the price — literally.

We all have reasons why we can't do things, but they're really just a different set of priorities. And people are allowed to have different sets of priorities. It's very rare, however, that we don't have a choice. We have a choice and this is what we're choosing.

It isn't that we don't have the money or the time — it's that we're bookmarking them for other things. It's not that you can't make *aliyah* or get married or travel or be mitzvah observant, it's that you choose not to compromise on the choices that would make these things possible. It's not that I can't eat healthy; it's that I love sugar.

This is an important differentiation because it's empowering to understand that you make the choices that determine your life. And it's also a responsibility. Nothing is actually, really an excuse; it's just a preference. And it's these preferences, choices, priorities, and deal-breaker issues that determine who we are, how we choose to live our lives, and how we determine how future generations will live theirs.

During the Spanish Inquisition, Jews in the Spanish Empire had a difficult choice to make. But they had a choice.

Of course, this works both ways. My dream as a young woman was to be in the theater. When I was twenty-four, I went to London with the idea of pursuing that dream. I got provisional equity based on my theater work in Israel and proceeded to try and realize that dream. Aside from the professional discouragement I encountered, I realized that to make that dream come true, I would have to compromise every other value and dream I had — a normal family life, religious observance . . . normal people. The price was too high. After only a little over two months in London, I went back to Montreal to study teaching. It was just not worth the price.

Our choices define us, not only who we are and what we value, but also who we are going to be and what our accomplishments and regrets are going to be.

Like Robert Frost's famous poem, it's the road we take that makes all the difference, and we get to choose what road that's going to be.

> *We are not human beings having a spiritual experience. We are spiritual beings having a human experience.*
>
> PIERRE TEILHARD DE CHARDIN

Sometimes I interact with people who seem very intelligent in other ways but don't seem to be able to accommodate the rationale of God or a higher being or a moral imperative not designed by humans. And I find this difficult to understand. I mean, I've known there's a God since I was a little girl. I always felt it and understood it to be true (however, my concept or service of Him has evolved).

And then it occurred to me that maybe you need spiritual intelligence to recognize Hashem and His Torah. There are of course people who are drawn to Judaism through the intellect or through emotions (so *kiruv* seminars instill heavy doses of both, along with *kugel* and *cholent* [two foods served on Shabbat] just to make sure the body doesn't feel neglected). But what if you also need spiritual intelligence to grasp the spiritual makeup of the universe, the way you need musical intelligence to hear the difference between a major and minor chord?

I looked up spiritual intelligence and, in fact, there has (more recently) been recognition of such a thing. However, while it includes concepts such as humility and compassion (admittedly spiritual values), there's not even a nod to God or any kind of higher being, no interrelationship with the universe, no ultimate purpose or any moral imperative. In other words, it's more metaphor than substance.

Maybe that's what is meant by *zechut avot*, that the merit of one's forefathers provides you with a spiritual type of inheritance and having that spiritual *yichus* (lineage) gives you the ability to recognize spiritual truth when presented with it.

But doesn't that go against the concept of the Jewish soul having a spark of the Divine within it and each of us being endowed with free choice to choose what's right and true, choosing the blessing and not the curse?

As Divine providence would have it, as I am writing this, I get a call from someone whom I used to be friends with. I had sent her something funny that she responded to by calling. As we caught up a bit, she cheerfully told me that her only son had gotten married a year previously to a Catholic girl whom he'd met at university. In Israel. This friend had made *aliyah* from Canada as an ardent and idealistic Zionist. Her siblings don't have any children. So in terms of Jewish continuity, with her son's intermarriage the link in her family's chain has been broken, severed . . . lost.

One of the reasons I'm not in touch with her anymore (her choice) is because of the disparity in our religious views. And for all her Israeli idealism, she is woefully spiritually unintelligent. I say unintelligent and not ignorant because she does know the basics of Judaism — she's had Shabbat dinner, she's been to synagogue, and she lives in Israel.

So how do we look at this phenomenon, Jews who are so removed from their Judaism that they intermarry, don't flinch if their children intermarry, and have no idea what the big deal is? Well, we can be angry, frustrated, appalled, even confused, but maybe the same way people are gifted or lacking in other types of intelligence, a person needs spiritual intelligence in order to recognize and come close to God. Their complete lack of comprehension about the real meaning of life and our place in it makes no sense otherwise.

And the same way we show compassion for people with other kinds of handicaps or deficits, maybe we can show compassion for them as well.

It won't change *them* but it will change *us*, and maybe that extra bit of *ahavat Yisrael* (love of a fellow Jew) will heal those suffering from being spiritually challenged, so that we endure fewer losses to our nation and less suffering overall.

First published in The Jewish Press

Lost in Translation

The single biggest problem in communication is the illusion that it has taken place.

GEORGE BERNARD SHAW

When I was twenty-three, I took a trip to Austria and Hungary. I spent five days in each. I had a wonderful time! Now this is the place to mention that, at least in 1983, Hungarians did not speak English. A few may have spoken a little English, but very few spoke any English. I had learned a few phrases in Hungarian before my trip, and that helped a bit. I had also learned to read the language, so if the sign said something I understood, I could understand what it said.

Hungarian bears no resemblance to any language other than Finnish. And I don't speak that either.

But I managed. I even managed to help an actress rehearse her lines in Hungarian. Because, if you'll remember, I could read it. I saw the musical *Cats* in Hungarian. I traveled by myself on the train to Szentendre.

On my last day in Budapest, I calmly took a taxi, with lots of time to spare, to the train station I had arrived at to take the train back to Vienna. I asked people what platform to take the train from. I slowly began to feel like Harry Potter looking for platform nine and three quarters, although I wouldn't be able to make that analogy for another fifteen years. Everyone was trying to tell me something about the train not being there and I doggedly held up the ticket to show them that yes it was. And then I finally understood.

There was another train station. And that's where my train was soon going to board. At the other end of Budapest.

Comprehension dawning, along with panic, I took another taxi and tried to convey the urgency to the driver of getting me to the station as quickly as possible. When I arrived, I asked where to board and with no argument, I was pointed to the platform where the train was then boarding.

My compartment companions looked a bit frightening to me, but I was so grateful to be going in the right direction, after I had been lost in translation.

Harav Kook vs. Don Quixote

Too much sanity may be madness. And maddest of all, to see life as it is and not as it should be!

MIGUEL DE CERVANTES

Don Quixote has been my favorite fictional character since I was young. And I knew who he was because that's what my mother named our hamster. I also have the right personality to emulate him — fighting injustice, pursuing romantic and idealistic love, seeking adventures and misadventures, fighting windmills...

Unfortunately, this propensity led to disillusionment, disappointment, and getting into fights and arguments a lot. Being quixotic had its down side.

But in my old age I've noticed that people don't become less stupid or irascible, more honest, kinder, or more disposed to do the right thing because you quarrel with them. You actually end up doing more harm than good. Mainly to yourself.

So I decided to try Rav Avraham Yitzchak HaKohen Kook's recipe for *tikkun olam* (rectification of the world):

"The purely righteous do not complain of the dark, but increase the light; they do not complain of evil, but increase justice; they do not complain of heresy, but increase faith; they do not complain of ignorance, but increase wisdom."

Because increasing light, justice, goodness, and faith is something that no one, no one, can argue with. So I'm not complaining!

Making Contact

Who is honored? He who honors others.

PIRKEI AVOT 4:1

My father suffered a heart attack while visiting Israel shortly before I got engaged. I went with my soon-to-be fiancé, who was studying at Sackler Medical School, to visit him at Ichilov Hospital.

A resident was taking care of my father, and I asked for information about his condition. He obnoxiously replied, "Why, are you a doctor?"

Without missing a beat, I said, "No, but my boyfriend is."

He immediately turned to Gordon, his attitude significantly more compliant, and started explaining his condition and, amazingly enough, I understood what he said.

In my early forties, I went to get a new pair of contact lenses (it turned out to be my last as I finally gave up on that particular vanity item due to the discomfort). The optometrist was young and very professional.

I began reading charts with her adjusting the lenses. She then said she would do a test on me to see if my eyes were dry. I know that test, I had my eyes examined only a few months earlier and I hate it, because it burns my eyes. "They're dry," I said. She didn't argue with me, didn't force me to do it. She just said okay.

Having completed my literacy test, and having passed with a grade of 6/6 (20/20), she then asked if I wanted my prescription made a bit higher to sharpen my vision or a bit lower to accommodate for my eventual

Making Contact

need for bifocals. I said no to both. Okay then, she said, I needed to put on two different lenses, stay with them for half an hour and then tell her what's more comfortable. I asked what I presumed was an academic question — if the lenses were disposable — and she answered that, no, they were sterilized and reused. I told her that I was not prepared to put on contact lenses that had been in someone else's eyes. This posed a problem. She told me that she couldn't give me an exact fit otherwise. Then she thought a minute and offered a couple of alternatives — either analyzing my old lenses or asking if the lenses could be returned if they weren't a perfect fit, or I could live with them if they came back half a number off.

What she basically did was honor me. She didn't argue that she was the professional and knew best or that I was being ridiculous (things I'd experienced before). She didn't tell me that I would have to pay an exorbitant fee to be accommodated or that I was ignorant of ophthalmological practices. She wasn't, like the aforementioned resident, patronizing or smug. She sincerely validated me and tried to respect my wishes. And when we went out into the waiting room for her to verify the options and have me pay, she stalwartly ignored the group of people vying for her attention and the woman who told her daughter to go into the examination room, even though the optometrist hadn't shown any sign of being through with me other than taking me into another room. I felt visible. I felt acknowledged. I felt respected.

The fact that this is so unusual and noteworthy points to a prevalent problem in our day and age. People are not generally listened to. They are not given credence as people worthy of an opinion. Doctors and professionals with letters after their names are often condescending. Service providers often regard their trade secrets as something no uninitiated novice could possibly understand. Teachers sometimes claim to know your child better than you do, and even strangers claim to know what's best for you and how and why you're not succeeding in your life's pursuits.

In one of Rabbi Abraham Twerski's books, he relates the story of a waitress who brought a little girl her order as she had requested it, not as her mother had amended it, and the little girl turned to her parents and said, "Look, she thinks I'm real."

We are starving for that kind of nourishment — people acknowledging the validity of our feelings, opinions, and rights to decide what is right for us.

It was such a pleasure to be treated like a "real" person. Although it was my vision being tested, I felt like I was the one who was truly being seen clearly.

First published in The Jewish Tribune UK

Ricki's List

When you make a to-do list, you should also make a to-not-do list.

BRIAN TRACY

I make lots of to-do lists and I love ticking items off them.

In my twenties, I had a good friend named Ricki. She was divorced with two kids and we studied in the same drama studio together. One day, I was driving with her and her kids. She was going away for a few days with a friend to Eilat, and she was running the errands she needed to do before she left. I remember this because she had a list. I even remember a few items on it. She had to stop at the library so her kids could return their books; she had to stop at the pharmacy and fill a prescription; she had to buy something. Maybe pay a parking ticket — she got a lot of those — and of course, drop her kids at her ex-husband's. There were about ten items on the list.

But as she was in a hurry and her flight was later than afternoon, there was no way she could do every item on her list. And she didn't. I was in awe!

For me lists are sacrosanct. The idea of her not completing something on her to-do list was inconceivable to me. And I started to feel stressed with the thought that she wouldn't.

She went to Eilat, had a great time with her friend, and did whatever she had to do when she got back.

And the world continued to revolve on its axis.

Mistress of Finance

Birds have bills, too, and they keep on singing.

I have been sparring with debt for the better part of three decades. Sometimes, I need to retire to my corner and seek succor. So I called my good friend Amy, who's known for her empathy and reframing ability. "But," I said, "I don't want empathy, I want 'Rah-Rah!' Give me hope and encouragement." I felt completely incapable of dealing with worrying about how I was going to cover another check.

She dutifully gave me the asked-for encouragement: how I could do it because I was doing it; how I always make it and how God always sends a timely miracle and I should trust that He will continue to do so. We discussed what I was dealing with and how I was coping, the brainstorms and Divine providence, the loans, the help of good friends and unexpected royalties that enabled me to make it to the next day, week, month. And then she said, "You're like a Master of Finance. You should be playing the stock market."

Although I hadn't been considering taking up another instrument, my spirits, head, and heart lifted. I had been transformed by that one sentence. I was no longer a struggling, devoted single mother, juggling a plethora of obligations, freelance jobs, and dreams. I was a Master of Finance, a wizard of Wall Street, a high player on the wheel of fortune.

I wrote it down as my new affirmation: *I am a Master of Finance.*

A Master's degree is conferred upon you by an academic institution when you have passed enough tests in a subject to show that you have achieved a certain level of mastery in it, learned the material, grown from it, and can even teach it to someone else. Each of our own trials and tribulations is our own personalized curriculum for achieving mastery in the area in which God wants us to gain proficiency. And when we do, others will seek out our counsel in drawing closer to the Dean of the University of Life.

While we are attaining our higher level of spiritual education, it is important as well to take electives in faith, courage, humor, and prayer. Then we will graduate with honors and make the Dean's list.

I know from personal experience that I have gained much of an education through my struggles with, and sometimes triumphs over, debt. Every struggle is full of meaning and all meaning makes life all the richer. I have shared this knowledge with others in the hopes that it would help them with their own struggles, so they would ultimately become the richer for it.

Because wealth is not determined by how much money you have but by how much knowledge you have and how you use that knowledge to enrich your life and the lives of others.

Reprinted from The Money Book

Going Overboard

> *Success is blocked by concentrating on it and planning for it.... Success is shy - it won't come out while you're watching.*
> — TENNESSEE WILLIAMS

There is a very delicately balanced equation regarding *hishtadlut*. You have to do enough but not too much, otherwise it works against you.

Trying too hard takes both God and other people out of the equation. It also keeps things in your life that have no place there anymore and leaves no room for the new things that do.

I have been a victim of over-*hishtadlut*. I've seen again and again (for me and other people) that when you try too hard, too long, too much, and it isn't meant to be, you lose.

Over-*hishtadlut*, as I understand it, is doing more than you feel comfortable doing to the point that you resent it; it's doing more than is considered the normal amount to achieve your goal (so the amount of effort would depend on what's normal in any given circumstance); it's believing that you are in control, not God, or that He's waiting for you to overextend yourself, which is sometimes true, but not always; it's ending up losing out because you tried so hard.

So let's say you work crazy hours to make more money when your time would be better spent elsewhere, and then you suddenly find you have a large car or dental repair. You run after a friendship or a *shidduch* (match) that isn't for you and you lose one that is. Over-*hishtadlut* can be what you do for other people as well. You try to convince others what's best for them to do. Then my smart friend Amy taught me the affirmation, "I don't have to take care of that."

There's a limit to how much we have to do in our own lives and in helping others. The problem, of course, is how you define the amount. Doing too little isn't good but doing too much can block the flow of abundance as well. If we overdo our *hishtadlut*, we suffer twice by not accessing our blessings and by doing things we never wanted to do.

Have you ever seen a child pushing a stroller? His mother has her hand on the bar and is "helping" him. Of course, it is really she who is pushing the stroller.

It is really God who is giving us our blessings. We just have to show that we want to receive them.

Seeking Forgiveness

> To forgive is to set a prisoner free and discover that the prisoner was you.
>
> LEWIS B. SMEDES

Most of us, I would venture, don't give forgiveness much thought, aside from the six weeks from Rosh Chodesh Elul to Sukkot, during which time we seek forgiveness for whatever wrongs, real or imagined, that we may have committed. I would like to think that six weeks of this a year is quite enough, but when I was forty-five years old, I discovered that perhaps that might not be the case.

I was having a lot of trouble making ends meet. I wasn't working, except for freelancing, and I didn't know where else I could cut corners. I decided to cancel the fifty-thousand-dollar life insurance policy I had for my ex-husband in case he couldn't pay child support. He was forty-eight years old, fit, slim, and perfectly healthy. It was just a couple of hundred shekels a month, but I figured it would help. In my last conversation with him, at the end of the conversation, I told him I had cancelled the insurance policy I had for him. "Don't die!" I joked.

Two months later, his father called me to deliver the sad and disturbing news that Gordon had died of a heart attack. Along with the thoughts racing through my head regarding my son sitting *shiva* and the unbearable pain to my in-laws, and all the things that had to be arranged quickly, was the life insurance policy I had cancelled.

Seeking Forgiveness

"Oh my God, I killed him!" I thought.

No one believed this. Especially since the money would have taken care of a great deal of debt. When you cancel insurance it takes a few weeks for it to actually be cancelled. The grace period had just run out.

Through the extreme kindness of my friends and neighbors, and my son's school, we weathered the *shiva*. My son returned to school and I went back to routine. Even before I thought to broach the subject with my in-laws — I mean how could I even broach the subject, it was heartless — my in-laws called and graciously assured me that they would continue to provide child support, at least until social security kicked in which, *baruch* Hashem, I found out I was eligible for. But I couldn't shake the feeling that Hashem was really trying to tell me something.

Twelve years before, when my father *z"l* died, I inherited some money. But then in quick succession I had a fire, a car accident, and a lawsuit for a million dollars that a buyer said he didn't owe me for the land in the aforementioned inheritance.

My friend works as the secretary at Netivot Olam Yeshiva in Bnei Brak. Thanks to our friendship, over the years, I have availed myself of the wisdom of the many holy rabbis there, and this time she thought I should go speak to Rav Aderet, one of the *mashgichim* (spiritual advisors), with a very good sense of humor and an even better sense of insight.

"What does Hashem want from me?" I asked him. First I lose a million-dollar court case that should have been open-and-shut, now this. I hadn't had a steady job for a year. I tried every *segulah* (auspicious action) for *parnassah* (livelihood) and nothing's helped. Of course, Hashem never lets me sink completely, and I am always grateful when an unexpected miracle occurs. There is always some salvation at the last minute from some unexpected place, but I am always left treading water. "I'm tired," I told him, with a dramatic sigh. "What am I not doing?"

I saw that the *rav* understood my pain; he understood my desire to do the right thing. He didn't lecture or judge me. Instead, he told a story.

He had been imprisoned in Russia for a year, when he had gone there to visit. While he was incarcerated, he too started wondering what he was supposed to be learning from this. He came up with the idea that if he had been separated from society, he must have done something against it, so he wrote letters upon letters asking people for forgiveness. Likewise, it seemed to him that someone somewhere had a grudge against me and that this grudge was blocking the flow of abundance to me.

"Pick ten people who might have some complaint against you and ask for forgiveness," he advised.

I was very upset. First of all, I have an overdeveloped sense of guilt as it is. It's unlikely that I hadn't already sought the forgiveness of anyone I may have thought that I had wronged, even in the slightest. Second of all, it seemed distinctly unfair. Here I was, a good, honest person. I gave charity, I'm not a sybarite, I try and do *chesed*, and yet someone could have a grudge against me and that could ruin my life?!

Yes.

I railed for a couple of days, but then I rallied. "Just do it," he had told me. Okay, if that's what it takes.

My first phone call gave me an otherworldly hint that maybe there was something to this theory. I had rented a bedsit in London over twenty years previously. For the unenlightened, a bedsit is a room you rent in someone's house and pay for by the week. When I planned to move out, a friend of mine was supposed to take over the room and was in charge of paying for it in advance. I returned one day to find my clothes being unceremoniously removed from the premises by the landlord because my friend had not paid and my lease was up.

Now, technically, I don't think I was responsible for paying this family, but it seemed like a good place to start. I had remembered the address and a friend in London looked up the number for me. The elderly lady picked up. She informed me that they had just gotten up from her late husband's *shiva*. She didn't remember either me or the incident, but she was grateful for my call and said that if I wanted to, I could give the money to charity.

"What if I give the money to a yeshiva and they can say *mishnayot* (verses from the Mishnah, the Oral Torah) and Kaddish (prayer to elevate the soul of the deceased) for your husband?" I asked.

She loved the idea. And so I sent a check to Netivot Olam for the equivalent of what I remembered one week in a bedsit cost. Providentially, it was the exact amount that the yeshiva takes for saying Kaddish and *mishnayot*.

They wrote the wife a letter informing her of the contribution, and I hoped that that had taken care of any unfinished business.

Then, I continued asking people for forgiveness. I only actually found one person who had a grudge against me, and it seemed so trivial that I wondered why anyone would bother to hold on to something like that for several years. It also showed me how easily people get offended.

Having completed my list of living people, I now had to ask forgiveness from the dead. It seems ironic that the one thing you can take with you to the grave is a grudge. So I called the rabbi from my childhood *shul* and asked him if he could please get a *minyan* (a quorum of ten men) together to go to my parents and ask for forgiveness in my name . . . in the snow. It was an unusual request, but he did it. He said he would get some yeshiva boys together to come with him. Again, providentially, a friend of mine in Montreal had sent me a check for $100. I told him I'd tear up the check and asked him to send another one for the same amount to the rabbi to pay the yeshiva boys, which was again exactly what it cost.

Nine months previously, Chabad had sent an emissary to the very non-religious neighborhood my ex-husband was from. He therefore merited to have the first *taharah* (purification) ever performed there. So I called the Chabad rabbi and asked him if he would take a *minyan* over to the cemetery for me. Well, getting a *minyan* together in this neighborhood was not the most realistic ambition. But again, providentially, the rabbi's relatives were coming for a visit, two of them rabbis in their own right, and three rabbis make a *beit din*. So they went over to my late ex-husband's grave and asked for forgiveness in my name. Chalk up another level of my spiritual growth that can be attributed to my ex. And look at all the *mitzvot* that accompanied him to The Next World!

So did all this help my financial situation?

Well, I didn't win the lottery or anything, though, to be fair, I didn't buy a ticket. However, while I was negotiating forgiveness in this world and The Next, I was hired, albeit temporarily, to replace a woman going on maternity leave for a few months. The timing did not escape me. And I did follow Rav Aderet's advice of not talking about it all the time and trying to be joyful, which has made my life a bit less stressful. And whether or not this was going to ultimately bring about a stream of salvation, I felt that I did my best to gain forgiveness and remove the grudges from the hearts of people I might have hurt.

But what this did more than anything else was reframe the whole issue of seeking and granting forgiveness. I learned that it isn't just a seasonal exercise in propriety. Bearing grudges is serious business; it can hurt people seriously and causes more than superficial rifts in relationships. People can take their pain to the grave and we can be held responsible. It's possible that no one, living or dead, really did bear me any grudge. Like I said, I really try hard to be a nice person. But perhaps, even if that's so, what Hashem wants from us, from all of us, is to make other people's feelings so much of a priority that we even feel our very sustenance depends upon it. Then we'll be very meticulous not to slight them in any way.

Every Yom Kippur, we hope to start again with a clean slate. We hope that we have been forgiven and that our forgiveness is sincere, and sincerely accepted. But any time is a good time to be magnanimous and seek and grant forgiveness. Though I'll admit that granting it is often harder than seeking it. Also, I think one needs to be wary of people who hold grudges. I think that's what's meant in the prayer by distancing yourself from someone of harsh judgment. Resentment doesn't do anybody any good. And graciousness doesn't do anybody any harm, so pursuing peace can only be beneficial to us.

So if anyone is angry at me for something, please forgive me. I simply can't bear any more grudges!

First published in Yated Ne'eman International
L'illui nishmat Rav Avraham Arieh ben Eliyahu David Aderet ztz"l

The Tipping Point

Despite our differences, we are one nation – a Jewish and democratic nation – with responsibility for each other and the right to demand tolerance from each other.

ISRAELI PRESIDENT REUVEN RIVLIN

Israel is a country you can cross in about eight hours, less now with Route 6, so most buses are intercity in that they traverse many cities on their routes. When you get on a bus, you have to say where you're going so you pay the right fare. As I was coming back from work one day in June, I got on the bus whose end destination was Ariel. Since I was talking on my cell phone to my son, I didn't state a destination, and the driver automatically took nine and a half shekels instead of six and a half shekels. When I pointed this out to him, he said it was my fault; I had been talking on my cell phone and didn't say I wanted Petach Tikvah. "Okay," I told him, "just change my ticket," and he refused.

Now, he could have easily given me another ticket and given my ticket to the person behind me or at the next stop but he didn't. He had an "I'm angry at the world" look on his face. I got indignant and told him I would report him to the bus company and he'd be fined. He didn't care. So after yelling at him a bit more, I made my way down the aisle and called the number on the headboard at the back of his seat. It wasn't the right number. And then I thought, "What am I doing?" There's a three-shekel (less than a dollar) difference. Why am I getting so agitated? And look how we're treating each other! I went back to the driver and said, "You know what, I'm not going to report you. This is a time we have to be nice to each other. I'm letting it go and let this be a merit for the boys to come home."

This happened during the second week of the captivity of yeshiva students Gil-Ad Shaer, Eyal Yifrah, and Naftali Fraenkel, a period where almost every moment people were doing something to help get the boys back — praying, sponsoring rallies and special evenings devoted to learning, delivering food to the soldiers searching, helping the families directly, writing articles, crying. In my thirty years in Israel I had never before seen such unity, and I often thought how overwhelmed the boys would be when they come back, *b'ezrat Hashem*, to see how much they had inspired — how much *chesed*, how many prayers, how much unity of every sector in Israeli society. I was convinced Mashiach himself would lead them home. And you never knew which one action, one compromise, one caring act, one extra prayer was going to tip the scales in their favor.

The driver didn't say anything, but something in his face changed. There are two interesting matters of *hashgachah* here. First of all, I saw the next day that I had called the wrong number. The customer service number was printed somewhere else and had I seen it, I might have gotten through. The other thing is this driver was Jewish. This is a line (Israel has about 700 bus companies) that usually is driven by an Arab. But I could see that this guy was Jewish.

The boys didn't come home again. And Mashiach didn't come. But if anything could have brought him it was the love and unity at the funeral of these three young heroes who had united the entire nation — first in hope, prayer, and kindness, and then in mourning.

Every year, we spend forty days (from Rosh Chodesh Elul to Yom Kippur) preparing for our day of judgment. And the same thing can be said of those eighteen days in June 2014. We never know what small thought, word, or deed is going to tip the scales in our favor. And so from Elul to Yom Kippur we work overtime to pile the merits and mitzvot on the scale so that we receive a favorable judgment and gain reprieve from any punishments coming to us. We usually do this on a personal level. But in June 2014, I saw it on a national level and that unity, that family devotion to one another, is what God wants. That unity tips the scales for everyone.

Tragically, devastatingly, the boys did not come home. They watched from their very special place in Heaven how hard we tried. And they, in their special place, watched while yeshiva students and soldiers, the secular and religious, politicians and rabbis, brothers and sisters sang and wept as they said goodbye. They weren't surprised because while we still struggle to understand, they no longer needed to.

Let us not forget the momentum that was created, that spiritual momentum that the mothers of the boys inspired, with their faith, their gratitude, their nobility, their courage when we all rose to the challenge of unprecedented kindness and unity.

These three wonderful boys — Gil-Ad Shaer, Eyal Yifrah, and Naftali Fraenkel — did something miraculous. They united us in an unprecedented way.

Let us continue to be one in the memory of these heroes, Naftali, Gil-Ad, and Eyal. May their memory be for a blessing and let us make them proud of us.

First published in The Jewish Press

Noteworthy Friends

You are the average of the five people you spend the most time with.

JIM ROHN

Some people are worth having fond memories of.

JAY LAWRENCE

Friends should come with instruction books.

On one of my birthdays a friend gave me, among other things, a small notebook. Notebooks are invaluable to writers, as Chekhov's character Trigorin in *The Seagull* demonstrates by making notes of anything of . . . er . . . note he comes across.

The notebook was sitting on my dining room table when I was having a conversation with my son, may he live and be well till 120, about my not giving him enough space. He was, at the time, after all twenty-three. "Okay," I relented. "Tell me exactly what you want me to do." I took the notebook and wrote down what he said, word for word, and read it back to him, which basically was that he wants my opinion and caring without directives, no telling him what to do, no words such as "should," "must," or "have to." Not an unreasonable request. For the next few days, I found myself cutting myself off mid-sentence a lot.

The next day, the friend who had given me the notebook called and told me that she didn't want to do something she had agreed to the previous day, as she was feeling ambivalent about it.

"But you said you would do it," I pointed out.

"Yes, well, you know," she said. "I don't like to disappoint people, so I say yes without thinking it through enough."

"But you're disappointing me now," I said. She began to defend herself and we were on the brink of an argument, so after she was done I said, "Look, let's make a deal. Whenever I suggest something or come up with an idea, let's remember to give you a day or two to mull it over before you say yes or no. That way you won't feel pressured into agreeing and I won't feel disappointed, okay?"

"Okay," she agreed. Then I took out the notebook and wrote it down.

In *Pirkei Avot* it says acquire for yourself a friend. But the literal meaning is: Buy yourself a friend. As we all know, anything you buy comes with an instruction leaflet. I am notorious for ignoring those instructions, either because they are obvious or too technical for me to understand anyway and who really needs all those functions? But people also come with a set of instructions, only you have to infer them or listen carefully when they are being explained to you. They range from technical things like "Don't call me after 10 o'clock at night" and "I'm allergic to milk," to more subtle things like "Don't forget my birthday" and "I'm afraid of moths." Being complex creations, people come with many more instructions than, say, your washing machine, and the consequences of ignoring them are usually greater.

It occurred to me that maybe we should all have such a frame of reference: A notebook with "handle with care" instructions regarding the quirks and sensitivities of our complex and intricate friends. Many of us keep a list of our friends' birthdays and the kinds of gifts they like to receive. What greater gift can there be than understanding, compassion, and sensitivity? So many arguments can be averted if we just listen when our friends express their pain and frustration at trying to make us understand when something we do or say or don't do or say bothers them. Our usual reaction is "Oh, you're too sensitive!" or "That's ridiculous! Why can't you be (fill in the blank)?" But we don't say that to our computer or our washing machine or our cell phone. Not if we want them to work. We do what we're supposed to. *Kal vachomer* with people. And don't we automatically do this when we need a favor? Don't we then use our intimate knowledge of people even subconsciously to sweet-talk them or curry favor?

Many years ago, a friend of mine who was having marital problems complained that her husband didn't listen to her. She would tell him what she wanted and needed, but she didn't feel heard. Then, he started keeping a notebook; a lexicon of what she meant when she said something. I don't remember how long he kept it up, but at least he made her feel that he was trying to understand her. And they didn't get divorced till many years later.

Mussar (ethics) teachers have urged us to do a *cheshbon nefesh* (personal accounting) every day. But perhaps it's not only our *nefesh* we have to do an accounting for. If we were to do an accounting for what is important to our friends, what brings them pleasure and what hurts them, and generally tried to understand them, it would be a lot easier to grant and gain forgiveness, which might then actually not even be necessary.

Just one addendum. *Ad valorem, bona fide* (according to the value, in good faith).

There will be friendships, relationships, and partnerships whose instruction manuals will be way too complicated to follow. And we should accept our limitations.

May we value our friends, our friendships, and our own instruction book.

First appeared in The Jewish Press

Slippery Slope

I've lived through some terrible things in my life, some of which actually happened.

MARK TWAIN

I'm a good girl. I try not to get into trouble. I like to have fun; I'm impulsive and spontaneous, but I'll always stop short of crossing red lines. Well, that's the plan anyway.

When I was in high school I had a deck of cards and I wanted to play with someone. But no one wanted to play. So I thought I'd make it more enticing. "Let's play poker," I suggested. Suddenly there were takers. So we played. For pennies and nickels and dimes. But the idea sort of took on a life of its own and, within days, our class resembled a small casino.

This was a Jewish day school in Montreal suburbia. *Es past nisht* (it isn't seemly). So the principal called me into the office as someone had generously pointed out that I had started the gambling spree.

Like I said, I toed the line and the principal realized I had gotten in over my head and he just told me to disband the casino. I, of course, complied and the class went back to playing bridge and 8-5-3.

Every year, we had ski day during our school's color war. It was a school trip so I always went. I don't ski, so I'd go tobogganing or walk in the snow, or freeze. One day, I went for a walk alone — a long walk. And then I got lost. In the woods. There was nothing in sight but grey skies, trees, and snow.

I had been following a road so I figured I'd try and double back. I don't really remember how I found my way back, only that I did, thank God. No one had noted my absence — which is a scary thought, but this happened in the 1970s.

One summer, in the early 1980s, I drove with a few people from the Student Ghetto in Montreal, where I was living, to Boston. I had studied there and was looking forward to visiting.

As we were a motley crew: two genders, five different nationalities, all in our twenties, driving a car that was sure to break down en route (it did), we were pulled over at the border and the car was searched. I wasn't too nervous as I had nothing to hide, but apparently a couple of the people whom I was with did. It was a great *chesed* of Hashem that the border police didn't discover the illegal substance that one of the group was smuggling into the United States. I could have ended up in jail, an experience I have not as yet had and would gladly eschew forever.

I have been in some other dangerous situations, which God has gotten me out of. I didn't mean to get into them in the first place, but naïveté and not thinking things through (but mostly naïveté) have led me to the precipice of disaster.

When we thank God for all the things, big and small, He's let happen, an even bigger thank you is merited for all the things He hasn't let happen and there are many, I'm sure, I'm not even aware of.

We can be so accident-prone, falling into situations that may not be our fault but are partially, at least, of our making.

I was volunteering at the AACI when a guy came in with a rambunctious toddler. This toddler wouldn't sit still for a second; he was all over the place and I remember thinking that the way that his father was trying to hold on to him strongly reminded me of someone trying to hold on to a ferret. Dad was chatting with me and someone else in the office while peeling his toddler off the wall and taking him down from the shelves he was climbing on, without missing a beat, the epitome of serenity, pulling him back from threat, destruction, or danger.

Isn't that what God's been doing for me? What He does for all of us? Constantly vigilant when we are not, neither slumbering nor sleeping and ever alert for another episode of bad judgment? I'm grateful for that protection and the knowledge it's there. Because, after all these years, I still tend to be woefully naïve.

Taken for a Ride

A learning experience is one of those things that says, "You know that thing you just did? Don't do that."

DOUGLAS ADAMS

I'm very much against hitchhiking and was very opposed when my son and his friends wanted to hitchhike as part of their backpacking trips. We're talking about hitchhiking in Israel. I only acquiesced when my son assured me they were doing it in pairs or groups, there's no other way to get where they're going, and they'd be very, very careful with whom they got in the car. I hate the whole thing. I didn't even hitchhike when I was young and more carefree and adventurous.

However, uncharacteristically, when funds were low and my son's vacation and mine intersected by a week and the North beckoned and I wanted my son to feel he had a cool mother, I said, let's hitchhike up north and you plan the route.

My son took a lot of pictures of me hitchhiking, with my *nouveau jeunesse* (or *clochard-esse*), much as you would an unusual natural phenomenon like a comet or a two-headed camel. Although he was a bit hesitant about the whole thing, he seemed to enjoy it. It was actually a lot of fun if not too big an adventure. We got a ride off the main highway with two young religious girls going north. While they were originally going northwest, they changed their mind and headed northeast to Kiryat Shmona, exactly where we were going. Couldn't have had better luck.

For the next couple of days, we hitchhiked back and forth from Metullah to Kiryat Shmona to the Jordan River, and my son kept snapping pictures of his hitchhiking mother. I was rather disappointed on the morning of the third day when he insisted we take the bus home, which was rather less fun, more uncomfortable, and more expensive.

A mere week later, I was waiting at the bus stop for my bus to work. A car with two middle-aged, religious Arab women stopped and asked for directions to the courthouse. As the courthouse was on my way to work, I said I'd direct them if they let me ride with them. It was two seconds after I closed the door that I realized what I was doing and was suddenly gripped by fear and awash with discomfort. This was not a good situation.

Oh well, I rationalized, it's unlikely that two middle-aged women who were on their way to the courthouse and just asking directions would be very dangerous. And after all, I volunteered to ride with them, I thought to myself, rather unconvincingly.

"Where are you from?" I asked, trying to sound casual, as they spoke between themselves in Arabic.

"Lod," one answered. Okay, that's pretty safe.

There seemed to be some confusion, however, as to whether they wanted the courthouse or the police station so I asked, in order to ascertain which it was most likely to be, why they were going there.

"Someone in our family has been arrested."

Ah.

"Okay, make a left at the next light and let me off at the bus stop," I said and then proceeded to direct them to the police station. I was relieved and shaking when I got out. I had in my hand the five-shekel coin I had intended to use for the bus and put it in the charity box of the synagogue near the bus stop.

I realized something, after my early morning adventure. When you try and change an inclination, a behavior, or a habit, whatever it may be, no matter how ingrained it is, and you take a step in the opposite direction, you never know how far you might end up the other way.

My experience that morning gave me a wake-up call and I reverted back to my more cautious and diffident ways regarding hitchhiking.

Yet it's illuminating to bear in mind that we can affect change in ourselves (for better or worse) just by taking one small step in the other direction. So we must be vigilant if we find ourselves slipping a little, and not try to delude ourselves that some principle we are being momentarily lax about is no big deal. And we must take heart and have hope that if we want to change some negative character trait or habit, all we have to do is lean a bit the other way, take one small step, and we're on the road to wherever we want to go. We just need to be careful whom we take a ride with.

Independence Day

Not all those who wander are lost.

J.R.R. TOLKIEN

I was doing my one-year post-graduate diploma in education. In general it was a fun degree, but the winter was dreary and I had some money my mother had left me, so I decided I'd use some of it for a midwinter trip to Florida.

There was a deal to Tampa, three hundred dollars for a week, including airfare, hotel, and car. It was very a good deal, even for the time, and I took it. The only problem was when I got to Tampa, I realized I didn't want to be there. I called a friend in Miami to ask if I could stay with her. She agreed. So I drove my rented car the first day to Fort Lauderdale and the following day to Miami.

It was as I was sitting in traffic on Alligator Alley, or some such road, that I realized that no one in the whole world knew where I was. I hadn't told anyone in Montreal of my change in plans. My friend knew I was coming to her but didn't know where I was exactly. It was a heady feeling.

My mother often told me about the car trip she, my uncle, and my father took with their Maltese dog (Lulu) across South America. It was in the 1950s and much more perilous than today. She told me that if you woke her up in the middle of the night and asked her to do the journey again, she would jump at the chance. My mother liked adventure.

So I wasn't exactly at the Panama Canal, but I did have this feeling of freedom, of adventure, of being incommunicado, and I liked it. It only lasted a day, but it was my Independence Day.

While I Was Sleeping

You achieve immortality not by building pyramids or statues – but by engraving your values on the hearts of your children, and they on theirs, so that our ancestors live on in us and we in our children, and so on until the end of time.
RABBI LORD JONATHAN SACKS

On my daily catch-up call with my son, Josh, at yeshiva, he casually told me what he had done the night before. He had ridden on a friend's motorcycle from Ra'anana to Herzliah (highway involved) to take a bus to Kever Yosef Hatzaddik (the grave of Joseph the Righteous) in Shchem. This trip took place between 10:00 p.m. and 4:00 a.m. (because during the day it's dangerous). Even as I was saying, "What?! Are you crazy?" I had to admit to myself (and in all fairness to him) that in my twenties, I would have taken a motorcycle ride in a heartbeat (which quickly would have accelerated with the motorcycle), and I was also rife with adventure, although *kivrei tzaddikim* wouldn't have been first on my list for adventure (although maybe in the middle of the night). Josh assured me that he was protected by the mitzvah. Which I'm sure covered the exhilarating ride down the highway with the wind rattling his teeth.

Now between 10:00 p.m. and 4:00 a.m., I was asleep, blissfully unaware of what dangers my son was exposing himself to. And when I recited Hallel on Rosh Chodesh (the new month) the morning following the conversation, I paused at the verse, "How can I repay Hashem for all His kindness to me?" (*Tehillim* 116:12). I realized that the reason I cannot repay Hashem's kindnesses, besides my limited mortality, is that there are a plethora of them I'm not even aware of, nor is anyone. In Israel, we routinely hear of terrorist plots that were thankfully and miraculously foiled at the last minute. But I'm sure that there are more that go unreported for reasons of security. How many times has it happened that we were at some place where moments later some tragedy took place that would have impacted on us had we not left moments before? And although my son did share his holy nocturnal adventures with me, I only found out after the fact. And thank God, *baruch Hashem*, everything was okay. But how many "adventures" do our families and friends partake of without sharing for fear of worrying us?

In our stressful and ever-mobile lives where dangers lurk on the pages of every newspaper, it feels like we should *bentch Gomel* (recite Birkat Hagomel) every time we return to home base.

I don't know how many people were sleeping when the drama of the ultimate plague played itself out in Egypt but like today, when not everyone makes it to the end of the *Seder* awake, I'd venture to guess that at least some of the nation, the oldest and youngest perhaps, were sleeping when God passed over their houses, shielding them from the Angel of Death and setting the stage for their redemption.

Even at the best of times, life is not free of calamity or crisis but like the well-known (Jewish) expression goes, "It could be a lot worse." This is not the soothsaying of pessimists but the realization that we have a lot to be thankful for, and God in His mercy watches over us and protects us from our worst fears, our worst enemies, and sometimes, ourselves.

I told my son that he has a very good reason not to consider buying a motorcycle; I would insist he'd take me for rides and I don't think he'd like that. No, he assured me, he wasn't as he knew someone who had just been injured in a delivery job and that was motivation enough. Oh yeah, and the brakes almost failed one time last night. "What!?!"

I asked my son not to do these things, but my request was half-hearted because at a certain age, we are all reckless and trust in our imperviousness and I know this. But I also know that my son trusts in Hashem and at the end of the day, whether we're sleeping in our beds or speeding down the highway of life or idealistically pursuing our spiritual quests, we are all dependent on Hashem's kindness and protection and most of the time, we too are blissfully unaware of how much we have to be thankful for.

Seder night is known as *leil shimurim*, a night of special protection, and we pray that as Hashem protected us on this night in Egypt, He continues to protect us, redeem us, and bestow His kindness upon us every day, and night, of the year.

First appeared in The Jewish Press
Reprinted in Eternally Grateful

Heartfelt Prayer

But I was prayer.

TEHILLIM 109:3

During Aseret Yemei Teshuvah (the days between Rosh Hashanah and Yom Kippur), my son and I went to visit my maternal grandparents, who are buried in two separate cemeteries in the Tel Aviv periphery.

My grandmother is buried in Nachalat Yitzchak in an area that borders Tel Aviv, Givatayim, and Ramat Gan. A kind of crossroads, appropriate to a cemetery. It turns out the Tzaddik of Shtefanesht (Ştefăneşti), Rebbe Avraham Matityahu Friedman, is buried there as well.

So after we visited my grandmother, we decided we'd stop in and say a prayer. As we were heading in that direction, an elderly woman stopped to ask us where the Rebbe's grave is. We pointed in the direction of the grave and followed after her. My son and I both said a prayer, while out of the corner of my eye, I was observing her.

She was leaning over the slab of stone, talking non-stop, with a cry in her voice. I wasn't even sure what language she was speaking, but she was pouring her heart out to the tzaddik as if she were unburdening herself to a trusted friend. It was completely sincere, pure, heartfelt prayer. The kind you aspire to and sometimes reach at *Ne'ilah* (the concluding prayer of Yom Kippur).

I told my son we can take a page from that woman's book (though she wasn't using one). He agreed wholeheartedly, and I knew that I probably got more merit from pointing her in the right direction so she could pray than from the prayers I uttered at the Tzaddik's grave.

Incognito

The honor of a princess is within ... in embroidered apparel she will be brought to the king.

TEHILLIM 45:14–15

Another job had come to an end. My colleagues had invited me to a farewell lunch, and as I approached the gate of my erstwhile employment, the guard asked to check my bag. I got annoyed. "What do you mean, 'check my bag?' I've been working here for two years. You've been saying. 'Good morning' to me several times a week for a year." He stammered and told me he had to check the bags of everyone he doesn't recognize. I let him peek into the depths of my handbag and entered the premises bemused and angry — until it dawned on me.

He *hadn't* recognized me. While I would usually slouch into work about 9:00 a.m. wearing glasses, a snood or kerchief and no makeup, I had shown up on this day in full regalia, wearing wig, contact lenses, makeup, and a "Let's do lunch" outfit. Since my contact with the guard had consisted of a fleeting glance and perfunctory nod, he based his recognition of me on external trappings and when he saw something different, it didn't jibe.

This is not an unusual occurrence for religious women, who may look almost unidentifiable from their domestic or work selves when they get all dressed up with somewhere to go. Someone once actually asked me for myself when they had seen me one way and come to the door encountering someone they thought was another person. And it happens to other women I know.

All this goes to show is how external appearances are misleading. They are so alterable that we can literally "become" someone else in a matter of minutes. We can change the cut and color of our hair or our wig; tinted contact lenses offer us an assortment of colors for our eyes; shoes can alter our height; and although losing weight is a challenge for most of us, gaining it certainly isn't. And the loss or gain of a couple of kilos also leaves its mark. Add to all that appearance-modifying accessories such as sunglasses, hats, and jewelry, and voilà! Even your best friend — or your own baby — wouldn't recognize you! Oh, but she would because to her, you are more than skin deep.

This same "now you see me, now you don't" description cannot be applied to the inner you. *Mussar* leaders have long discussed the difficulty of changing even one character trait. Among *ba'alei teshuvah*, the "easiest" thing to change is their dress. You can be *shomer Shabbos* (Shabbat observant) for merely one week, but if you're wearing long sleeves and a high neckline you're seen, at least at eye-level, as belonging.

Our external appearance in terms of our clothes and our looks says little about the real us. It is ephemeral and a reflection of our fickle and fashion-addicted natures. Even our physical appearance, though it may reveal something of the soul it envelops, both changes over time and becomes insignificant to people with whom we've forged deep bonds.

The true "us," the "we" that matters, finds expression in our thoughts, our words, our deeds, and those inexpressible feelings that are between us, ourselves, and Hashem.

I went back a few minutes later to explain to the guard what I understood had happened, but he once again explained that he had to check those people whom he did not recognize, apparently still not realizing who I was.

We must get to know others in terms of who they are inside so that we recognize more than their wrappings and, of course, we must also seek to recognize our true selves.

First printed in Yated Ne'eman International

The Meaning of Life Is Cuddling

Cuddling literally kills depression, relieves anxiety, and strengthens the immune system.

Unofficially, I would say that the pictures most liked, shared, and likely to elicit a smile on Facebook or any social media are pictures of interspecies cuddling — two, usually furry, creatures in repose and embrace. Ditto for YouTube videos. And why is that? Because cuddling is a fundamental need. Because closeness to any creature brings us serenity, fulfillment and, by extension, closeness with Hashem. If I think about it, memories of cuddling are among my best memories. Isn't our earliest memory walking around cuddling a stuffed animal? I still have mine, Lala, my stuffed bear. She looks the worse for wear but she still shares my bed.

Any activity that brings you physical and emotional closeness with a relative, friend, or pet, and is an expression of warmth, love, affection, vulnerability, and sharing the earth with a fellow creature is vital to our existence. Cuddling, snuggling, hugging, sharing are what provide universal oxytocin for our emotional, physical, and spiritual survival. If we have caviar but we're eating it alone, it leaves a bad taste in our mouths. And the really amazing thing that the images of these interspecies acts of affection teach us is that they don't have to occur with a spouse (the one!), our best friend, or even someone of our own species.

My neighborhood features a clowder of cats that are in residence in the park and around the cluster of stores in my neighborhood. Most of them don't let you touch them. But one ginger cat has taken up residence near the post office. He sits on the bench outside and lets everyone and anyone pet him, all day. And they do. This cat has learned the secret of life.

Cuddling is the simplest pleasure, and although we can't lie on the hearthrug all day and sleep in the arms of our favorite furry creature, we can take time, and make time, for this important activity. Because from armadillos to zebras, from grandparents to babies, we can all use a hug.

Thomas and Friends

It's not what you look at that matters, it's what you see.
HENRY DAVID THOREAU

When I was in school in Montreal, some decades ago, we had a lice scare. All of a sudden, schools were discovered to have unwanted visitors. How lice can survive in thirty-degrees-below-zero weather, I'll never know, but it is a generally held belief that if we ever, God forbid, have a nuclear holocaust, the cockroaches and lice would survive to found a new world. Anyway, back in Montreal, I escaped the lice scare without a scratch.

In Israel, too, I never had a louse in the house, even after I was blessed with a child. Regular lice checks in *gan* (kindergarten) reported him clean and clear. It was I who discovered the first louse in my hair.

It was in 1993 and I panicked. I went out and bought one of those chemical rinses you put on your hair and a fine lice comb and I stood in front of the mirror on lice patrol, being totally disgusted and freaked out about the six-legged creature clinging to my follicles.

That was until my son started school and, from first grade on, lice tended to get into our hair and like Nechamah, the lice heroine of the Israeli children's book, my lice would play tennis with my son's lice when we cuddled.

I stopped buying the chemicals and started to accept lice searches as par for the course in bringing up a child in Israel.

Then one day, a friend gave me a new perspective on this Middle-Eastern phenomenon. She told me that she calls her children's lice "Thomas and his family." So she'd go, "Oh look! Here is Thomas's uncle!" or "I just found Thomas's second cousin." Matching her mock enthusiasm, I started doing the same thing with my son.

One day, my friend and I were talking on the phone and I told her that Thomas had come to visit us (Thomas gets around) and he had thrown an anniversary party for his grandparents. There was a big to-do and lots of friends and family came. But you know how it is with some guests — they never know when to leave.

King Solomon sent us to observe the animals and learn from them. While it is true, he never sent us specifically to the primates, if we were to observe the monkeys, we'd notice how for them, looking for lice is a bonding ritual.

I took their cue and my son would lean on me and play Tetris, or read a book, while I searched for Thomas's family tree. And oddly enough, I came to enjoy this ritual as a relaxing way to be close to my son. It even became kind of addictive, like a game in which you try to find as many lice (or lice eggs) as possible and better your score.

This activity also forced me to stop running around and sit still spending a "lice" time with my child. While it's true that many mothers have many children, *baruch Hashem*, and while lice multiply exponentially, a mother's time decreases exponentially. Therefore, were mothers to spend fifteen minutes a day, with each child, combing for lice, they'd have little time for anything else. But if we have to do it anyway, we might as well make it a pleasant experience.

As with everything in life, *Chazal's* (our Sages) dictum that how you view a situation defines the experience, applies here, too. Discovering Thomas and his family made me closer to mine.

I guess I became a thoroughly integrated Israeli when it comes to lice because I no longer consider their trying to get a head as something lousy. As Thomas would say, it helps me and my son stick together.

First printed in Yated Ne'eman International

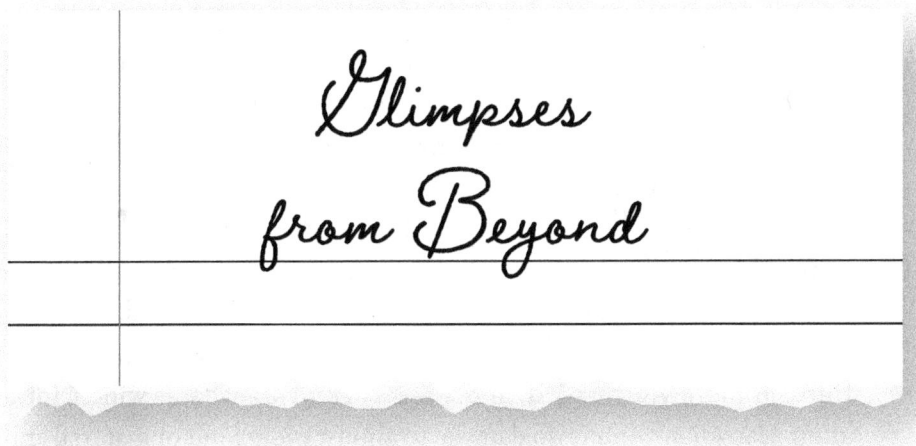

Glimpses from Beyond

Death ends a life, not a relationship.

MITCH ALBOM

My mother *a"h* died just before my twenty-first birthday. I saw her twice before they buried her, once in the hospital, and once at the funeral home, and it was then that I was convinced with a hundred percent certainty that each of us has a soul. Because hers was no longer with her. She looked like a wax rendition of herself and I knew that her true self had gone to the world beyond.

I have a fondness for frogs; I'm not sure why. When I was little, I used to delight at the frogs I'd find in the garden on autumn evenings when my mother and I would go out to play with our St. Bernard.

Not long after my mother died, I was sitting on campus talking with a friend and I mentioned that it had been a long time since I had seen a frog.

The next day, I went to the cemetery to visit my mother's grave and I saw some movement on the mound of earth. I looked closely and it was a frog. I have never before, or since, seen a frog in a cemetery. What's more, it was summer, and the dirt on the grave was dry (frogs like wet earth). I had no idea where it had come from, but I had no doubt that it was my mother's sense of humor winking at me from beyond.

Many years later, I was visiting Montreal with my son. Twenty years had gone by since my mother's death. I took him to see our old house. It had changed hands three times, I'd heard. Everything was different. The bushes had been taken away, my mother's rose beds were gone, the windows and doors had been changed, and it was painted a different color.

There was only one vestige from my childhood. My mother had made a birdhouse for the birds in winter. She had built it herself and had tied it to the maple tree on our front lawn with a braided rope (our St. Bernard Aurora's old leash). The birdhouse was gone but that rope was still there. I had sold the house ten years earlier, soon after my father had died, but none of the owners had removed the rope (and it was quite an eyesore).

Thirteen more years passed, and I was back in Canada in winter for a wedding. Canadian winters do damage to almost every kind of material and structure, and repairs are frequently made on homes after the winter's devastation.

The rope was still there, testimony to the kindness my mother had demonstrated to God's creatures and perhaps a reminder to me that the mitzvah of that kindness survives for eternity.

In June 2019, I flew in from Israel to attend another wedding in Montreal. The first day there, I went to visit my parents and uncle at the cemetery. When I approached my mother's grave I saw there was a seashell on top of it. There are no seashells in Montreal, the city is hundreds of miles from the nearest ocean, and there was no one to visit my mother's grave but me.

We connect with the ones we've loved and lost through memories, pictures, and the mitzvahs we do to elevate their souls. But occasionally, if we're vigilant, we will see them connecting with us as well.

Parts of this article appeared in From This World to the Next, A Portion of Kindness, and Drawing Closer

Driving Test

If we can learn from everything, what can we learn from a taxi? Humility — for if you want to get in, you have to lower yourself.

REBBE AHARON OF BELZ

I have always had a problem with Israeli taxi drivers. I fight with them.

One Motza'ei Shabbat, after spending Shabbat at a friend's, I took a taxi home and, as usual, had a fight with the taxi driver. My son, may he live and be well, till 120, had been sick on Shabbat, and I was not in the mood for the cabbie's shenanigans.

Sunday morning my son was still sick. His temperature was 101.2. There was a Purim party at school he was going to miss.

I get stressed out when my son is sick, especially when he's going to miss his second-grade Purim party. I didn't know what to do. Then it came to me. I said to my son, to myself, and to God, "I take it upon myself, *bli neder* (without making a vow), not to fight with any more taxi drivers, and in this merit, may my son get well and not be sick anymore."

Fifteen minutes later, my son went to throw up. "I think my fever's gone," he said. I took his temperature. 98.6. I checked to make sure the thermometer wasn't broken. I took it again. Same thing. We went to the Purim party.

Three days later, I had occasion to take five taxis. The first taxi was no problem. In the second, the driver wouldn't put on the meter. The person I was with told him he had to put on the meter according to the law. I didn't get involved. "I don't argue with taxi drivers anymore," I said. The driver turned on the meter.

The test came in the third taxi. We got into the cab, my son and I. I told the driver the street I wanted in Petach Tikvah. The taxi driver wouldn't put on the meter.

"Fifty shekels," he said.

"Okay," I said.

We started to drive.

"Where's the seatbelt?"

"You don't need one in a taxi."

I controlled myself and laughed. My son laughed because I was controlling myself.

The taxi driver didn't know where to go. I told him to ask on the two-way radio. "It's illegal," he told me. I used his cellular phone to call a friend to get directions. The driver warned me that his phone card was running out.

Since the beginning of the ride, he'd been eating sunflower seeds with one hand and driving with the other, when he wasn't playing with the controls on the radio.

"Where are we going?" my son asked. I didn't remember. I got a vague idea from my friend's son of where the street we were looking for was and told the driver. He still didn't know how to get there but told me it would cost another fifteen shekels.

"But I asked you to turn on the meter, and I told you where I wanted to go when I got in the taxi," I said.

"Mommy," my son said with a smile, reminding me, as I had asked him to do. I told my son I loved him.

"Okay," I said to the driver. "You get us to where we need to go. Anyway you have to, and when we get there, you tell me how much you want me to pay you." It didn't sound like me, but since I was the only woman in the cab, I assume it was me who said it.

The taxi driver asked directions a few times and got us there. He was still eating sunflower seeds when I asked, "How much do I owe you?"

"Fifty shekels," he said.

Driving Test

The fourth cab driver appeared the second I began to look for one. He put on the meter.

The fifth cab driver insisted on returning change to me. Okay, that last part's not true. But it could be.

First published in Horizons Magazine

The Play's the Thing

There's no business like show business.

IRVING BERLIN

In my early twenties, before I became religious, I performed in both amateur and professional theater. I auditioned on Broadway, in an open call for *My Fair Lady*. It was an adventure but a disaster. I even got provisional equity in London, based on my theater work in Israel, which meant that were I to be cast in a West End production, I would be eligible to perform in it. But I didn't stick around London long enough to find out. A combination of disillusionment and the lack of sunshine in springtime Britain drove me to other countries and alternative pursuits. Theater in London also didn't have the family atmosphere of theater in Israel.

Then I turned thirty, became religious, and had a child within a very short time span, which ostensibly put an end to my theater career. But when I was forty-five, a friend asked me if I would be interested in a small part in the Bnei Brak women's English theater group. So I accepted.

When we got to the theater for our first performance, I walked out on the stage for the first time in fifteen years. It was familiar but different. For one thing, I was a little less blinded by the limelight. I discovered that a lot of things about doing a play with only women were the same — the camaraderie, erratic rehearsals, fears about forgetting your lines, lines from the play that became running jokes and quoted whenever possible, the excitement, the willingness to watch the same scenes over and over again, the sheer pleasure of doing something creative and fun. The costumes, makeup, props, and scenery were all in place — at least most of the time — and the adrenalin rush was there, surging us to great heights and great high notes we didn't reach in rehearsals. There were the technical glitches, the fluffed lines, and the humorous improvisations attempted to cover for them that are part and parcel of any performance.

But there were things that were very different from conventional plays, even before the pre-show *dvar Torah* (Torah thought) and chapter of *Tehillim*. Although there were definitely leading roles, there were no stars; there were no egos. There was the good feeling that we were doing something as much for others as for ourselves; the proceeds of the performances were going to *tzedakah*, for example.

Since there were no intrigues, political or otherwise, nor backstage romances, there was less tension. There was, of course, the adherence to *halachah* (Jewish law), at all times, and a scrupulous adherence to modesty, even though we were all women performing for all women. There was care not speak *lashon hara*. There were the *brachot* before going on stage in a scene that involved food, which of course conformed to all stringencies of *kashrut*. There was significantly more eating backstage as well.

And there were babies. That definitely was not a part of my previous theater experience — women nursing them during intermission and babysitters keeping them quiet during the performance. I found my best audience in one of those babies, whom I entertained while her mother was changing. All the women became surrogate mothers when they weren't being actresses.

Though all-women religious theater might be lacking some of the glamour of conventional theater, it certainly had the requisite talent and professionalism. And we had encouraging and appreciative audiences. And it was not only an artistic endeavor, it was a spiritual pursuit, driven not by ego, not by ambition, not by perfectionism, but by the pure intent of religious women, giving of their precious time, using their God-given talents, to serve Hashem and their community. We all had a good time.

Though I don't know what kind of reviews our group would have garnered on Broadway, or in the West End, the audiences were enthusiastic with their praise, and I hope that in the celestial balcony, there was only thunderous applause and a Heavenly voice shouting, "Encore!"

First published in The Jewish Tribune UK

Hard to Admit

More people would learn from their mistakes if they weren't so busy denying them.

HAROLD J. SMITH

I was working as a secretary at a law office. On the same floor were at least two other law offices. My boss dealt with civil law — bankruptcy, civil disputes, that kind of thing. And I wondered, on more than one occasion, why is it that people can't admit they're wrong, that they've made a mistake? It would make life so much easier for them as well as the other parties involved.

I've made mistakes in my life. I remember many years ago writing an article that said, among other things, that people who haven't gotten married by forty for the first time would probably never get married. Then, years later, I flew to Montreal to attend the wedding of my best friend, who got married for the first time at fifty-four.

As a teenager, I championed women's causes. I remember at seventeen taking a class in Women's Studies with a very feminist teacher. I felt kind of like a hypocrite when, during this time, I participated in a beauty contest. I would not do either again.

We all make mistakes, we change, we grow, we learn, but the one thing that we don't seem to be able to do is admit we're wrong. Aside from *ba'alei teshuvah* and that whole journey. It seems to be easier to say we've made a mistake and lived our lives the entirely wrong way but now we've seen the light, than it does to say we're sorry we're late and it's our fault, not the traffic's.

I had an unpleasant series of interactions with people I was working with on a project. We had made an agreement and they were not fulfilling their part of it. It wasn't out of malice or bad intent; it was the result of a few bad judgment calls and overcommitment. What frustrated me more than the result, which I was pretty frustrated with, was their total inability to say, "You know what? You're right, I made a mistake. I'm really sorry; let's fix this." Instead they accused me of insensitivity and being difficult. I admit I'm not pleasant when I'm angry, but why can't people just say they made a mistake, they're sorry? Why? It adds more than insult to injury, and that's one of the major reasons people get into such conflict.

It's an ego thing. In a good way. People don't like to feel that they have done something wrong. People want to uphold their image in their own eyes as good people, as honest people, and when they can't deliver on a promise or on a check or on an agreement, they will find a way to excuse their behavior and blame the other person. And the irony is that it's so much easier to forgive when someone makes a mistake and is willing to make amends.

But no, they're late because there was traffic; the check bounced because they weren't paid on time; they can't meet the deadline because they don't have the manpower; they couldn't keep their promise because they were just too busy . . .

All these excuses might be true, but they do nothing to appease the person who was slighted or to fix the situation. And when people don't own up to their mistakes, when they don't take responsibility for their bad calls, they make them again and again, as well as the same excuses.

While I was contemplating this on the bus, stewing in my righteous anger about the above-mentioned incident, I looked up and saw graffitied on the wall facing me, two inches from my nose, *Tohav kemo sheatah soneh* (Love the same way that you hate). Only in Israel does God give you *mussar* while you're sitting on the bus.

So maybe the other side of this is there would be less conflict and litigation, if we took just a little bit less offense and let go of our righteous anger, even if it is justified. Maybe we should understand that God runs the show, and the irritation, discomfort, and insult we suffer is really from Him. Maybe we need to focus on our response to the offense and not only the other person's responsibility, which is really *their* responsibility, because there is always the possibility that down the line, we'll reconsider and feel we were wrong.

The question is, though . . . will we admit it?

First published in The Jewish Press

Let It Rain

Life isn't about waiting for the storm to pass. It's about learning how to dance in the rain.

VIVIAN GREENE

I have always loved the rain. Especially summer rain. One of my favorite memories is of being a teenager and going to get ice cream with my friend, Marcy. We got caught in the rain on the walk back to her house. We were drenched. I was delighted!

In Israel it doesn't rain in the summer. In Israel rain equals winter. In all my decades here, I have never been able to convince anyone that what Israelis call winter is actually fall and that winter involves snow and below-zero weather.

I remember waiting for my son to get off the school bus one day and it started to rain. I was sitting on a curb with an umbrella and didn't move. I got drenched. I was laughing. The people in my neighborhood must have thought I'd gone crazy.

My last trip to Montreal was for a wedding in the summer. The evening I arrived, I left the restaurant I had gone to with friends and a light rain started. I danced with glee. Then I explained to the people near me why I was whooping about the rain; that it doesn't rain in Israel in summer. Turns out they were in from the States for the same wedding.

I used to go Israeli folk dancing on Mount Royal (near Beaver Lake) in the summers on Tuesday evenings. Sometimes it would rain and then only the folk dance fanatics would continue dancing. I remember dancing to *Hora Mamtera* ("The Sprinkler Dance") in the rain.

Rain is mysterious, romantic, calming, comforting, refreshing, and cleansing. It's one of my favorite smells.

When we say the Prayer for Rain on Shemini Atzeret, I always get emotional. Also when saying the Prayer for Dew on the last day of Pesach. The transition of the seasons always moves me. But I look forward to the rain like a parched flower. Maybe it's because I'm named after a flower.

So, I don't need to learn how to dance in the rain. I've been doing it since I was three.

Tears on My Pillow

Life is time sensitive.

Although most people call me an optimist and cheerful (and I've often wondered why), my default emotional expression is crying. I cry when I'm happy, sad, angry, frustrated, moved, proud, touched, grateful . . . you get the idea. I read somewhere not long ago that there are people whose tear-duct sensors are near their nerve endings . . . anyway there's some sort of biological reason for this. Also I'm an HSP, a highly sensitive person.

One of my key tear triggers is milestones. Not just marriages, *brits*, funerals, and birthdays, but any act marking a transition — annulling and burning the *chametz* before Pesach, Tashlich, the shofar signaling the end of Yom Kippur, the Prayer for Rain, the Prayer for Dew, anything that marks an end and/or a beginning.

These things make me cry because they symbolize, to me, that we've made it again around the year. We've come full circle. We've survived and that's something significant and meaningful to celebrate.

But isn't that equally true every time we wake up? Isn't every moment, every experience a transition to the next, a beginning and an end, meaningful in its own way? Yes, I realize we can't live like that. And frankly, it's hard to even live like I do. But aren't we all looking for exciting adventures and meaningful experiences? Isn't this why we study, travel, dream, create, and aim higher in our aspirations?

When my son was sitting *shiva* for his father, I sat there crying too and one visitor said that tears were the river of life, or some such thing.

I sail down that river, daily, and I watch as the scenery changes, yet still stays the same.

From a Different Perspective

You can't change the people around you, but you can change the people around you.

One of my father's brothers *z"l* lived in Chicago and once every year or two, we would drive down to visit him and his family. The other two brothers lived in Australia, so it was a bit far for a visit. I've never yet actually been to Australia. But I have pet a kangaroo.

When I was about thirteen or fourteen years old, we drove down to Chicago where my cousin Renée was working as a counselor in a day camp. Everyone of course thought it was a good idea for me to go along and help her. I don't know how much help I was, but I spent the day with her in the camp, which was fun.

Afterward, Renée told me how much the other girls liked me and how they told her she had a really nice cousin. This wasn't what I was used to. I was not popular at school, and suddenly being so popular bolstered as well as confused my self-confidence. Like a radio signal that was scrambled.

Over the course of my life, I've been the recipient of much contradictory information about myself — criticized and acclaimed in equal, extreme, and paradoxical doses.

Whether it was my acting, singing, dancing, personality, character, writing, friendship, social skills, sense of humor, attractiveness, grace, academic performance, religiosity — everything was either torn apart or praised to the skies. That could make anyone nuts or at least very self-conscious.

But then I learned that people see what you reflect back to them about themselves. Also context is important, as well as how capable the other person is of judging you. We have to consider the source, the situation, and the timing.

My life changed when I left high school and I had more freedom in choosing my social and academic circles, in which I found my many niches.

Sometimes, even often, we're put in places where we would do better not to be. But for the first years of our lives, no one actually consults us.

Sometimes we put ourselves into situations— examinations, job interviews, competitions and contests, auditions — where being judged is par for the course. The only thing I can tell myself is that if I wasn't accepted, it's because my destiny was not meant to play out in that particular context. I was meant to be somewhere else for some reason. It's not necessarily a reflection of any flaw in me.

But there *are* times we choose to put ourselves in situations with people who don't value us, who don't appreciate us and who treat us accordingly, not because we deserve to be treated that way but, perhaps, because they are not worthy of us. Or the situation is just not healthy for us or who we're meant to be.

That hope we sometimes harbor that the other person will regret not having married us, published us, hired us, or remained our friend, won't materialize simply because the other person is simply not capable of recognizing our inherent value.

I've never liked funhouses. Seeing myself distorted is not what I consider fun. I think regular mirrors are enough to contend with. But that's what I've done every single time I've allowed myself to be in the company of someone who sees me through their negative, warped, or uncomprehending lens. And many times, I have chosen to actually pursue these people, to consider myself honored to be in their company. That's not a good option.

When people say glibly, "It's not you, it's me," they're not dismissing you with a cliché, they're being remarkably honest. Because most of the time it is in fact them, not you. Or it may be that someone doesn't bring out the best in you, which is kind of like a double reflection, also prevalent in funhouses.

So now, I've learned, as much as possible, to try and choose the company and friendship of those who see me as wonderful and valuable, not only to satisfy my ego and because it's more pleasant, but because that means they're wonderful and valuable themselves. And that's not only the best company to keep, it's company that will help me recognize and become my best self. Now that's fun!

Zoology

Someone told me it's all happening at the zoo.

PAUL SIMON

I love animals. This is a love I inherited from my mother *a"h*. I have a picture of her at Yellowstone National Park with a bear cub standing on its hind legs with its front paws on her leg. This was taken moments before she spotted the mother bear and ran for her life.

Once I was teaching high school and one of the students, hoping to scare me, had a small snake peeking out of his sleeve. I did scream, but what I screamed was, "Oh, he's so cute! Can I hold him?"

I have attempted many things, short of becoming a veterinarian (I had neither the temperament nor the biology grade), in order to bring me closer to what Hagrid would call *interestin' creatures*.

Once, I wrote an article for *The Jewish Press* about the Biblical Zoo in Jerusalem, having spent a day following around the veterinarian in the hope of realizing my lifelong dream of petting a lion and hugging a bear, but the closest I got was petting an injured bat.

A couple of times, I tried to get a job as a tour guide at the Safari (a zoo in Ramat Gan that also has a wildlife component reminiscent of the Serengeti). But the first time my presentation on sloths was a bit, um, languid. The second time, when I had everyone get up on chairs and pretend they're giraffes, went really well, but then I was told I was too old for the job. At that time I still had my age on my resumé. Couldn't they have just deduced that?

On one furlough from work (aka period of unemployment), I decided to try to volunteer for the Safari. My first stint was with the small apes. I followed around a twenty-three-year-old *olah* (immigrant) from Baltimore, who had studied care of creatures in captivity (not to be confused with Fantastic Beasts and Where to Find Them), who was living her dream of caring for them despite being laid up for six months after an orangutan injured her hand (not on purpose, of course).

The first thing I did was to trip over a root and fall in the capuchin cage. A capuchin out in the yard looked in, and I laughed at the irony of him watching my antics in the cage as he gamboled outside.

I spent less than three hours helping feeding the monkeys and clean their cages and I was exhausted. But it was exhilarating work! And I had the rare thrill of getting really close to a gorilla, but thankfully not too close. I couldn't watch him though because they don't like eye contact. I did have the pleasure of scratching a chimp's back (under strict supervision). She turned around and offered her hand in thanks. Her name was Lychee.

The staff leader saw my plight and suggested I volunteer with a less taxing department. But I never went back as a volunteer. I just went back to writing articles. The aquarium was next. I wanted to see an octopus, but he was hiding.

I can understand completely why the Garden of Eden was paradise (the animals without the work). The zoo is my happy go-to place. It's where I feel closest to God. Well, closer than in a shul, because the miracles of creation are spread out before me, explained to me, and sometimes interact with me.

My bucket list has many places where animals roam free. But until I can get to them, I continue to admire the wildlife I have access to in my neighborhood. You'd be surprised how many species you can find in Petach Tikvah.

Dress Code

We read off the many signals that our companions' clothes transmit to us in every social encounter. In this way, clothing is as much a part of human body language as gestures, facial expressions and postures. Even those people who insist that they despise attention to clothing, and dress as casually as possible, are making quite specific comments on their social roles and their attitudes towards the culture in which they live.

DESMOND MORRIS

When I attended McGill University, I went roller skating with a friend. But when we got there we discovered that there was a "no jeans" rule. I was wearing jeans but I thought the rule was ridiculous, so I complied with the rule in a way that meant I wouldn't have to leave. It was winter, so I tied my bulky coat around my waist and took my jeans off. They couldn't kick me out, because I wasn't wearing jeans. The poor guy working there chased me around the rink, trying to get me to put on a pair of pants that were too big for me, and who knew how many people had worn before me. My friend was impressed.

Fast-forward ten years, I was newly married and driving with my new husband, Gordon, from Los Angeles to New York, where he would be doing his internship. It was crazy; we did it in six days. We stopped in Texas for supper at a "swanky" French restaurant where we were met by a stuck-up maître d', who snobbishly informed us we couldn't enter because there was a dress code. My husband had to wear a jacket and me a skirt. As all our luggage was in the trunk of our car, there was no problem in our changing. We donned the appropriate attire and entered the mostly empty restaurant where the waiter long-sufferingly took our order. I was tempted to order in French, assuming he didn't know any, but I resisted the urge.

A few years later, I had taken my son to Los Angeles to visit his father, my now ex-husband. We were at a baseball game where the Angels were playing a visiting team from New York. To accommodate the kosher New Yorkers in the stands, the L.A. Stadium had kosher hot dogs, which tore Gordon's attention away from the game. "I gotta see this," he said.

But the game was memorable for another reason besides even the hot dogs. It was the first time I was recognized by my attire as an Orthodox Jew. A woman saw me as I was headed for the bathroom, and she asked me if I knew where the kosher hot dog stand was. That's how I knew it was there. The only reason she would have asked me is because my clothes gave me away as an Orthodox Jew. I was recognized as one of the "in" crowd, for being a religious Jew.

I had mixed feelings about that identification. It kind of meant forever leaving a part of myself behind. But clothes are a uniform and I was for the first time recognized as a soldier in Hashem's army or, to be more in sync with the context, part of the winning team.

My religious dress made more of a statement than tying a coat around my waist to roller skate, or changing into a skirt to gain admittance to a snooty restaurant. It broadcast who I was and what I believed. And I didn't have to change a thing.

Fame and Anonymity

How wonderful it is that nobody need wait a single moment before starting to improve the world.

ANNE FRANK

When I was twenty-seven, I played Ann Frank's sister, Margo, in the play *The Diary of Anne Frank* at the Saidye Bronfman Centre in Montreal. This is a difficult part to play because she's on stage throughout the play but has only twelve lines. And knowing that this is a real person you're portraying makes it all the more difficult. It's a sad play. More so because this particular production was cursed. One of the actors died, the one who replaced him broke his ankle, I replaced another girl who had to back out because of other commitments, and snowstorms had a big effect on the numbers in our audiences.

Anyway, one night backstage, I said to one of the older actors, "I want to be famous!" He looked at me quite seriously and said, "No. You don't want to be famous, you want to do something that will make you famous." I looked at him and said, "You understand me!" It was one of those rare times in my life when I felt totally understood.

As I got older, I found I preferred being less in the limelight; being a stage manager or a playwright held more appeal for me. They allowed for greater creativity and were less stressful.

I remember when I wrote regularly for *The Jewish Tribune* in London, I would go to a *simchah* and there would be British people there. I would introduce myself, and they would say, "Oh, are you the Rosally who writes for *The Jewish Tribune*?" I would smile demurely and they would gush.

One day, I had occasion to call some woman somewhere in England about something and right on cue, she gushed. The same day, I called *The Jewish Press* in New York to ask them if they would be interested in my writing for them.

"Who are you?" They asked. I answered. "Never heard of you." Fame is a fickle friend. Thankfully, that was just a little glitch; I've been writing for them for the better part of twenty-five years.

But my thespian colleague was right. It wasn't fame, not the limelight I wanted, it was doing something that made a difference. Writing has the right balance between fame and anonymity, well, more so before the Internet. But still. Someone could have loved a book I've written but wouldn't recognize me if I were standing right beside them. And sometimes, I even give up my byline for a good cause.

Whether you like fame or anonymity, being a writer gives you the best of both worlds. And writing is very important. *The Diary of Anne Frank* is one of the world's most important and popular books.

In the Pink

> *Color is all. When color is right, form is right. Color is everything, color is vibration like music; everything is vibration.*
> — MARC CHAGALL

In the early 1980s, I gave my friend, for a birthday present, a makeover at *Color Me Beautiful*. That's a place where they swatch you with colors, tell you what season you are, and present you with a palette of your most flattering colors. The bonus was I got to surreptitiously find out what color palette suits me as well.

Chromatic science tells us that colors have a big influence in our lives. They affect our mood, how we are perceived by others, even our health. Our favorite colors also tell much about our personalities, our interests, and our type of spirituality.

Doesn't the Torah spend many verses describing the colors of the fabrics used in the Mishkan (Tabernacle)? And isn't nature full of amazing and brilliant colors and hues?

To go back to the swatching, she was a Winter and I was a Summer, and since then, she has worn her winter colors and I my summer.

I was at a writer's conference, many years ago, and as we registered, they handed out plastic folders. I was given a yellow one. "Can I have pink?" I asked. The lady smiled and graciously gave me the pink.

Kids aren't being spoiled when they want something in a certain color. The certain color speaks to them; it makes them feel happy and connected.

About a decade ago, I asked my son to come with me to help me pick out a new phone. He is much more tech savvy than I am. Children of his generation were born that way. And he's also much more of an economic maven, so I figured I'd let him choose the best phone at the best price. The salesperson brought out a few phones.

"Oh, oh, I want this one! Oh, it's purple!" I exclaimed.

"So much for technology," my son muttered.

It was a compact flip phone (this was before cellular phones belonged to generations) of a beautiful shade of purple and I loved it!

Color is a language that speaks volumes, and clearly is an issue that is not black and white.

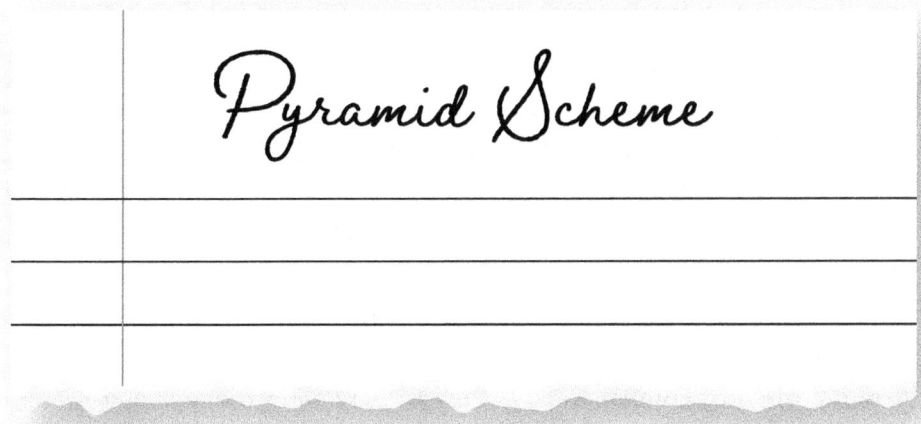

Pyramid Scheme

> *The consequence of a mitzvah is a mitzvah, and the consequence of a sin is a sin.*
>
> PIRKEI AVOT 4:2

One of the most popular entrepreneurial inventions of our time is the pyramid scheme. The way this works (and often doesn't) is that each person who joins the company signs up under someone else, who benefits from the sales the new person makes; the latter in turn tries to get others to join the scheme so that he can thereby benefit from any sales his protégés make. If this works, everyone stands to gain. Unfortunately, each person's success is dependent upon the initiative of the people under them. If they are successful, the higher-ups stand to make a lot of money. If they don't, then the one who signs them up doesn't reap any benefits.

I have no intention of discussing the merits or drawbacks of this particular system. I only wish to point out that this is neither new nor a solely economic brainchild. The system exists in Judaism and has been around a long time. And it's a lot more successful on a spiritual plane than is its economic counterpart.

The way it works is this: Say you do a mitzvah and this inspires someone else to do a mitzvah. Not only do they get the reward, but so do you. You will also reap the reward of any subsequent mitzvahs performed down the line due to the influence of your initial one.

Many years ago, I went to a seminar sponsored by Arachim, a well-known *kiruv* organization. I was inspired to do this by a friend who had herself been encouraged by her aunt, who had also attended. Had this been a company, my friend's aunt would long ago have been promoted to upper management.

The ripples we make in the spiritual world are counted, and we reap the reward in this world and The Next, even after we have long ago lost count of the people whose lives we have touched, inspired, or influenced. Celestial bookkeeping is technologically more advanced than the bookkeeping of any pyramid-oriented company, and the rewards are many times greater.

One reads countless stories of people who have found their way back to Judaism because of a comment they heard or a scene they witnessed, even though the protagonists who made the impression never knew of their effect on the *ba'al teshuvah*.

We must always be aware of the significance of our words and actions. We are part of a very influential team of entrepreneurs, marketing the most important product in the world — our spiritual legacy. That's one pyramid that's a true wonder of the world.

First published in Yated Ne'eman International

Glossary

A"h: Acronym for *alav/aleiha hashalom* (may he/she rest in peace)

Ad 120: Till 120

Ahavat Yisrael: Love of a fellow Jew

Aliyah: Immigration to Israel

Aseret Yemei Teshuvah: The ten days of repentance between Rosh Hashanah and Yom Kippur

Ba'al Teshuvah: A returnee to Judaism (plural, *ba'alei teshuvah*)

B'ezrat Hashem: With God's help or God-willing

B'hiddur: On a high level of beauty

Baruch Hashem: Thank God

Bashert: Soul mate

Bat: Daughter or daughter of

Bein Hazmanim: Intersession at yeshiva

Beit Din: A court made up of three rabbis to render a verdict on various issues

Beit Din Shel Ma'alah: The Heavenly Tribunal

Beit Hamikdash: The Holy Temple

Ben: Son or son of

Bentch Gomel: Recite *Birkat Hagomel*

Birkat Hagomel: The prayer of thanksgiving said after surviving a dangerous or life-threatening experience

Bitachon: Trust

Bli Ayin Hara: Without the evil eye

Bli Neder: Without making a vow

Brachah: Blessing (plural, *brachot*)

Brit: Circumcision; ceremony at which a circumcision is performed

Chag: Holiday, festival

Chalav Yisrael: A dairy product containing milk that was milked under the supervision of a religiously observant Jew

Chametz: Any product containing leavened dough, which is forbidden to eat on Passover

Chanukah: Festival of Lights

Chesed: Loving kindness, benevolence

Cheshbon Nefesh: A spiritual accounting

Cholent: Stew eaten on Shabbat, also known as *chamin*

Chuppah: Wedding canopy or ceremony

David Hamelech: King David

Derech Eretz: Proper, refined behavior

Dvar Torah: A Torah discourse

Eliyahu Hanavi: Elijah the prophet

Elul: The last month of the Jewish calendar year

Emunah: Faith

Erev: Evening

Es Past Nisht: It isn't seemly; it doesn't go over well

Eshet Chayil: Literally, a woman of valor; a liturgical poem, based on Proverbs 31:10–31, read at the Friday night meal in honor of the woman of the house

Gabbai: Synagogue sexton (plural, *gabba'im*)

Gan: Kindergarten

Gedolei Hador: Religious leaders of the generation

Gemach: A charitable organization that provides free or low-cost goods or services

Genizah: A special repository for holy books and writings

Giyoret: Feminine form of *ger*, a convert to Judaism

Hakarat Hatov: Gratitude (literally, recognizing the good)

Halachah: Jewish law

Hallel: A prayer, praising God, comprising Psalms 113 to 118, recited on festivals

Hamelech: The King

Hashem: God (literally, the Name)

Hashgachah Pratit: Divine providence

Hechsher: Kosher certification

Hishtadlut: Effort

Hoshea: The prophet Hosea

Illui Neshamah: Elevation of the soul

Kaddish: The Mourner's Prayer, recited in praise of God, which is said to elevate the soul of the deceased

Kal Vachomer: A fortiori (with greater reason)

Kallah: Bride

Kashrut: Kosher level or certification

Kever Yosef Hatzaddik: The grave of Joseph the Righteous

Kiddush: Blessing over wine on the Sabbath and festivals

Kiddush Hashem: The sanctification of God's name

Kinneret: The Sea of Galilee

Kippah: Skullcap

Kiruv: Jewish outreach to bring people closer to Judaism

Kivrei Tzaddikim: Graves of the Righteous

Klal Yisrael: The Jewish People

Kollel: A yeshiva for married men

Kotel: The Western Wall

Lashon Hara: Evil speech; e.g., gossip, slander

Leil Shimurim: A night of protection

L'havdil: Said when distinguishing something holy from something profane in the same example (literally, to separate from)

Ma'aser: A tenth of one's earnings given to charity

Mashgiach: Spiritual advisor

Mashiach: The Messiah

Melaveh Malkah: Meal eaten after Shabbat (literally, accompanying the Queen)

Middot: Character traits

Midrash: Textual interpretation of the Torah

Midrashic: From the Midrash

Mishkan: The Tabernacle, which, in the desert, was the predecessor of the Temple in Jerusalem

Mishlei: The Book of Proverbs

Mishnayot: Verses from the Mishnah, the Oral Torah

Mitzvot: Commandments; also refers to good deeds

Motza'ei: The night after (Shabbat or a festival)

Mussar: Ethical advice

Nachas: The pride and joy typically felt by parents, grandparents, and teachers

Nahafochu: The situation was turned on its head

Nefesh: The animal part of the soul

Ne'ilah: Concluding prayer of Yom Kippur

Nero Ya'ir: May his light shine

Neshamah: Soul

Neshamah Yeterah: Additional soul people get over Shabbat

Nisayon: Test or trial

Nishmat Kol Chai: A prayer in which every living thing praises God (literally, the soul of every living being)

Oleh/Olah: An immigrant to Israel

Parnassah: Livelihood

Pesach: Passover

Pftoo, Pftoo, Pftoo: Onomatopoeia of spitting on the evil eye

Pirkei Avot: Ethics of the Fathers

Purim: Holiday celebrating how Queen Esther saved the Jews of Persia from the wicked Haman, who wanted to annihilate them

Rachmana Litzlan: May God have mercy

Rav: Rabbi

Rebbe: Chassidic rabbi

Rosh Chodesh: The new month

Rosh Hashanah: The Jewish New Year

Rosh Yeshiva: The head of a yeshiva

Segulah: An auspicious action meant to bring good fortune

Seudah: Festive meal

Seudat Hodayah: Feast of thanksgiving

Sha'atnez: Forbidden mixture of linen and wool

Shabbat/Shabbos: The Sabbath

Shabbat Kallah: The celebrations for a bride on the Sabbath before her wedding

Shalom Zachor: A ceremony/party welcoming a newborn baby boy into the world the Friday night before his *brit*

Shechinah: The feminine aspect of God's presence

Shemini Atzeret: A holiday following Sukkot

Shemirat Halashon: Guarding one's speech from slander, gossip, etc.

Shemot: The second book of the Torah: Exodus

Sheva Brachot: Seven blessings recited during the wedding ceremony; also, the week of marriage over seven days of celebrations named for them

Shidduch: Match

Shiur: Class, usually on a religious topic

Shiva: A period of seven days of mourning

Shlomo Hamelech: King Solomon

Shomer Shabbos: Sabbath observant

Shul: Synagogue

Simchah: Celebration or happiness

Siyum: A celebration marking the completion of study of a section of Torah, Mishnah, Gemara, or other religious text

Sugya: Topic under religious debate (like in the Talmud)

Sukkah: A temporary booth in which Jews eat and sleep during the holiday of Sukkot

Sukkot: Feast of Booths

Taharah: Purification of a body before burial

Tanya: An early work of Chassidic philosophy written by Rabbi Shneur Zalman of Liadi, the founder of Chabad Chassidism, and the main work of the Chabad philosophy and approach to Chassidic mysticism

Tashlich: A ritual of casting one's sins into the water, performed on Rosh Hashanah

Tefillin: Phylacteries (two small square boxes containing Torah passages and worn during morning prayer services)

Tehillim: Psalms

Tikkun: Rectification

Tikkun Olam: Rectification of the world

Tzaddik/ah: A righteous man/woman

Tzedakah: Charity

Tzitzit: Ritual fringes worn on a four-cornered garment

Yehudah v'Shomron: Judah and Samaria

Yetzer Hara: The evil inclination

Yichus: Lineage

Yishuv: Settlement; the settlement of the Land of Israel before the State was declared, primarily in the eighteenth and nineteenth centuries

Z"l: Acronym for *zichrono/a/am livracha* (may his/her/their memory be for a blessing)

Ztz"l: Acronym for *zecher tzaddik livracha* (may the tzaddik's memory be for a blessing)

Zechut Avot: The merit of one's forefathers

www.ingramcontent.com/pod-product-compliance
Lightning Source LLC
Chambersburg PA
CBHW050521170426
43201CB00013B/2038